to have all the material needs touched my heart and actually brought a tear in my eye. About those who do not have shelter, food and clothing, the author narration of what she observed serves as a reminder of how we take for granted to things we have. The Therapist reminded me that we could give from the little we have, which is far more than others have. Other life lessons that I take from the book are practicing present moment concentration to help one reach the peak - more like taking one day at a time - the importance of living in the moment as opposed to just living life running from one task to another. The author has covered this very well, and I trust that readers will find this beneficial.

The use of mountains to describe life challenges and how we seek solitude during difficult times speaks to me, and now I understand why hiking especially solitude moments is what some people yearn for to escape from busy life activities and have moments to reflect. I like how the author balances this with service to the people because one can never find complete healing just in solitude. We have to serve others even during the most difficult moments in our life. What stands out for me is also the emphasis on not only climbing the physical mountains but understanding that we again "climb our proverbial mountain as well to reach the pinnacle of our life purpose".

Monique is full of wisdom, and the book is a true reflection; she is a person who always affirms and inspires others. This book is well worth reading.

**—Veronica Ntsiea**.

# Teacher on the

# Mount

By

Monique M. Keller

# REVIEWS FOR
## Teacher on the Mount

This is a provocative book that takes the reader on an interesting journey through the lives of three women and the inter-related growth in their relationships with each other and most importantly with their Triune God of Father Son and Holy Spirit. It is about 'listening' to God's voice in a modern frenetic world. It is also about dealing with the hardships and challenges of life through our relationship with God.

The author simplifies/converts complex issues into understandable concepts and principles using the provocative imagery of mountains as a metaphor to illustrate how we can enhance our ascending relationship with God. She uses everyday life lessons interwoven with relevant and appropriate biblical scriptures which enhance the story. Simply told, the story gives birth to new conceptions of the wonder of our triune God.

—**Robin Joubert**, Honorary Associate Professor at *UKZN OT Dept* and Lay Minister and licensed preacher at St *Thomas Anglican Church Berea, Durban.*

\*\*\*

*'Teacher on the Mount'*…….what a simplistic, yet interesting and personal way to relate the personal mountains faced off some of the most famous figures in the bible. The author has taken the proverbial leap of faith to unashamedly share her personal spiritual journey in listening to that voice which calls us for great things. This book tells a story of a beautiful spiritual journey full of twists and turns but eventually experiencing the calm and peace that is found in the Teacher on

the Mount.

It reminds me of the saying "Everyone sees your glory, but no-one knows your story". Your story of trials and tribulation might go unnoticed by many, but the joy of reaping the fruits of your labor is indescribable.

**—Mercia Patience**.

\*\*\*

The author of *Teacher on the Mount* is an expert in seeing the divine in everyday life. In this book she highlights that ordinary encounters e.g. therapist-patient or nurse-patient interaction could turn out to be life changing. A *Teacher* or *Mentor* destined to support and guide one to achieve one's dreams and goals may be just around the corner if one is willing to see, listen and accept this offering of the universe. The author shares her knowledge and understanding of the divine by linking her life experiences, in some instances uniquely South African, with scripture thereby making scripture understandable and relevant to present-day.

The book is a pleasure to read with short chapters which focus on specific life events to underscore scripture implications. I am convinced that the book will inspire and encourage readers to look at life differently and climb their proverbial mountain.

**—Ronel Roos**.

\*\*\*

Teacher on the Mount is filled with general life lessons where the content inspires one to continue to be a better person despite life challenges. The description of the difficulties people experiences, from homeless people to individuals who seem

*Teacher on the Mount*

Published by KHARIS PUBLISHING, imprint of KHARIS MEDIA LLC.

Copyright © 2021 Monique M. Keller

ISBN-13: 978-1-946277-93-0

ISBN-10: 1-946277-93-2

Library of Congress Control Number: 2020952686

All rights reserved. This book or parts thereof may not be reproduced in any form, stored in a retrieval system, or transmitted in any form by any means - electronic, mechanical, photocopy, recording, or otherwise - without prior written permission of the publisher, except as provided by United States of America copyright law.

All New and Old Testament Scripture quotations were taken from The New King James Version of the Bible. Copyright © 1979, 1980, 1982 by Thomas Nelson Publishers.

Descent in Hell (Part II) a part of The Gospel of Nicodemus, Acts of Pilate is from "The Apocrypha New Testament" M.R James, Translation and Notes Oxford: Clarendon Press, 1924. Accessed from www.earlychristianwritings.com.

The poem Paradise Lost by John Milton, 1667, Book I: Lines 27-83.

All KHARIS PUBLISHING products are available at special quantity discounts for bulk purchase for sales promotions, premiums, fundraising, and educational needs. For details, contact:

Kharis Media LLC
Tel: 1-479-599-8657
**support@kharispublishing.com**
**www.kharispublishing.com**

# Dedication

I want to dedicate Teacher on the Mount to Paul, my dear husband, and Linda and Pieter, my parents.

I know that the curiosity and determination I have is because of your consistent support and love, which fuels my Spirit to pursue what is and what could be.

To my editor, Nikki Solomon, thank you for your patience and support.

# TABLE OF CONTENTS

|    | Dedication | Vi |
|----|------------|----|
| 1  | Therapist | 1 |
| 2  | Hospital | 5 |
| 3  | A Call from the Burning Bush | 10 |
| 4  | The Call to Help Others | 22 |
| 5  | Travelling Home | 33 |
| 6  | Book in the Ward | 37 |
| 7  | Trauma in the City | 44 |
| 8  | John the Baptist's Death | 48 |
| 9  | The Mentor | 55 |
| 10 | The Therapist and the Mountaineering YouTube | 61 |
| 11 | The Manager and Hades | 64 |
| 12 | Manager and Joseph | 72 |
| 13 | Mentor Teaches on Road trips | 79 |
| 14 | Everest Mountaineering Clothing and Equipment | 84 |
| 15 | Darkness in Hades | 91 |

| 16 | Final list | 99 |
| 17 | Reaching Your Everest | 100 |
| 18 | Heir of Fire | 111 |
| 19 | Mountaineering Techniques | 118 |
| 20 | Teacher on the Mount | 127 |
| 21 | Reaching the Highest Mountains Within Yourself | 133 |

# Chapter 1

## Therapist

The cold morning breeze is fresh, with the promise of a new season in the air. Winter in some regions of South Africa is cold, but Winter in Johannesburg never reaches below -5 degrees Celsius. Temperatures are never low enough for it to snow, a fact that makes Abigail grateful as she takes her daily drive through the heart of the City of Gold.

Abigail Grace, a woman in her late thirties, is wearing her favorite work attire: black scrub top, comfortable slacks, and her always comfortable, bright-red sneakers adorning her feet as she steps on the brake. Off the highway and approaching the infamous dangers of the City of Gold, she removes her cell phone from its conveniently-mounted position to her left on the windscreen and places it in the compartment in her door.

It's been eight months since she commenced her postgraduate research; there are eight studies and during these early morning drives to the hospital she does much of her research. She plays downloaded YouTube videos on her phone which allows her to beat the boredom of the 40-minute, always-congested drive to work. More important, the drive itself allows her to learn more about her current field of postgraduate studies. In the last month, two specific topics have posed the greatest challenge: Research methodology and statistical methods in research.

## *Teacher on the Mount*

Abigail has not always had an easy life, but she has accepted the offer of a new work opportunity. This internship at a world-renowned university gives her a challenge and new meaning in life. Over the past months, she has faced challenges that have stimulated and rejuvenated her weary soul.

A professorial voice bellows from the hidden cellular phone: "If the distribution shape, plotted as the x-axis showing the different values, and the y-axis as the occurrence frequency, follows a bell-shaped curve, therefore, the data are normally distributed."

She hears this and drives on, feeling as confused about research on this day as she always has.

Her little white Toyota Etios drives effortlessly on the straight, smoothly tarred road, but it suddenly inclines and she comes to a stop at a red robot. Looking upwards, as if seeing them for the very first time, Abigail's eyes scan upward to grey skyscrapers towering over the city. Then, she shifts her attention to the popular bridge situated next to the Ponte, a well-known high-rise apartment building. The iron-strong bridge in the wake of the infamous Ponte was built many years ago. At that time, the engineers who designed it could not possibly have known that the bridge would become the haven for many hungry, desperate people.

The change from Winter to Spring takes a few weeks before the early mornings shed their chill, and for the people sleeping under the bridge, whom Abigail sees clearly from her current position, it is still bitterly cold. A blanket is a luxury. Sleeping bags are a rare sight. For the first time, she sees beyond the homeless and focuses on the decay and suffering in which they shiver. It is the kind of suffering no person can foresee.

Is this a new awareness dawning on the more-present person? She asks herself, *Are the drivers of the cars even aware of the desperate people they are passing?*

In the early, cold hours of this new day, the sun rises and soon shines brightly. People start emerging from their make-do beds. Abigail notices the newspaper-filled black-bag pillows, flattened cardboard-box beds, and newspaper blankets. The sight is difficult for the green-eyed, soft-hearted woman; a feeling of helplessness rises within her. Her heart breaks as she soon loses count of the numbers of men, women, and children who have made this area their homes. People of all ages live under the bridge. The only common factor is their ability to endure hardship.

Some of the men are already up at 6:30 am and are busy plying their trade of washing windscreens as cars stop at a red robot. This is their only way to make money for their daily bread and maybe a drink to dull the aches of their unfulfilled lives.

Abigail spots a dirty, old, once-red couch which is falling apart. The splash of color seems out of place in the bare greyness under the bridge.

A young boy still sleeps on a folded cardboard box. It is almost certain he doesn't attend school. Instead, he probably spends his days begging for food or money to help his family or feed himself. She fights back tears that spring up as she thinks about the difficulties these people face for something as small as a piece of bread. Gratitude fills her, as well, as she thinks of her work, the food she can buy, the roof over her head, and the comforts of her home.

At the go signal, she accelerates slowly away from the bridge, her Toyota inclining to reach a peak and plateaus for 50 meters and then descending.

"The bell curve of plotted data indicates a normal distribution," the professor continues and Abigail experiences an "aha moment." She exclaims, "The road I just travelled was a bell-shaped curve! Will the people living under the bridge ever move out and reach a better life, a peak, the top of the bell curve?"

# Chapter 2

# Hospital

The silver-haired lady is tired and lies in her hospital bed. Entering her room, Abigail, now the Therapist, is concerned at being called in to see this lady a day early. The orthopedic specialist is in quiet conversation with the ward manager.

"Good morning," Abigail says, her voice chirpy and a smile on her face.

"I didn't have a good night's rest, you know," the silver-haired lady states.

Abigail replies, "I'm sorry to hear you didn't sleep well. I believe you are scheduled for a knee replacement today. Was it anxiety that kept you awake?"

"No, dear, not at all! I had a dream about my future which made me decide to cancel my operation."

The doctor beckons the shocked therapist, and the ward manager shakes her head as she leaves the room. The clearly exasperated doctor says, "I and the ward manager both have tried to convince her to go ahead with the operation, but she keeps refusing because a dream told her not to. Please give it one more try. If she still refuses, you will need to give her home exercises to help with her mobility and manage her pain." Abigail nods as she glances at the lady. "Who would do such a thing?" the doctor mumbles, almost inaudibly, as he leaves the room.

Abigail returns to the old lady, who is lying on her back with her eyes closed. She hesitates before speaking.

"Ma'am, are you sure about cancelling your operation?" she asks. "You've waited so long for a new knee. As you're aware, the waiting list is quite long. You finally made it, and today is your day. There is no guarantee you will be put on the waiting list again."

"That won't be necessary. I won't have the operation today or in the future," the lady responds resolutely.

"If you're sure, I will inform the doctor. He just wanted me to ask you one last time," Abigail states. She leaves the room and chats briefly with the doctor and the ward manager before returning.

She says to the old lady, "The ward manager will start preparing your discharge papers, and this could take a couple of hours. In the meantime, I will show you some exercises you can do at home to strengthen the muscles around your knee and hip." With a clear tone of warning, she continues, "This will help with your mobility and assist with pain management, but please note that it will not fix your knee."

"I'm aware," the old lady smiles, revealing teeth too unnaturally white to be anything but false. The smile fades briefly, and the lady says, "I'm so sorry to be so difficult. I am aware of the preparation that went into organizing this operation, and I have not only wasted staff time, but I have also wasted operating room time. I do hope they manage to get someone else into surgery earlier. However, I am certain about my decision." That snowy white smile returns.

There are more questions than answers about this determined old lady, but she is content and relieved with the outcome of her hospital visit. Although curious, Abigail starts with a subjective assessment of silver-haired Mrs. Watkins.

She says, "Ma'am, I believe you had a knee replacement on your other leg, is that correct?"

"Yes, dear. Several years ago. It was the best decision I ever made. It was a modern operation which improved the quality of my life and allowed me to walk long distances. I was even able to climb more mountains with my son, which was wonderful. Not big mountains, granted, but the smaller ones can be just as beautiful and rewarding," Mrs. Watkins answers, her thoughts replaying a fond memory.

"May I ask you something before we begin?" Abigail asks, now more confused about the situation. She has dealt with patients who were ecstatic after a successful operation and, months down the line, have a new lease on life. She has also dealt with patients who have had to suffer incredible pain as they waited for their turn to have the operation they need. In the city of Gauteng, a long waiting list – more than 1000 people – to have a knee replacement is common. She has never dealt with a patient who has willingly decided to continue with their limited mobility and sometimes excruciating pain.

"Of course, my dear," the silver-haired lady answers.

"How is it that you so confidently cancelled your operation just because of a dream?"

"To answer such a question takes time, dear. How

much do you have? There is no quick and easy explanation for making a life-changing decision from a mere dream. Much is needed for any one person to understand fully that I'm not a crazy old woman." With a chuckle, the old lady continues, "I need your full attention. If you have somewhere else to be, I can't explain my decision."

Intrigue consumes Abigail, and she says, "For now, I am all yours. I am supposed to be giving you a full home-exercise regimen, and it will take a while, as you need to practice each set of exercises." Her curiosity growing, she continues, "I had nothing else planned and, since I am an intern, I expect they won't schedule anything further for me today. I had planned to leave early anyway. May we talk while we go through the exercises?"

"Certainly, my dear. That would be wonderful," Mrs. Watkins says.

Abigail pulls the orange curtain around the bed and explains the first part of the exercise regimen. She sits in the chair next to the bed as the old lady follows her instructions.

As she moves and repeats and follows the guidelines, the old lady begins, "What I'm about to share with you doesn't only come from joyous high moments where I felt like I could see for miles and my path was easy, but it also comes from painful, low moments when I felt I couldn't see my destination and my path was rocky. I have experienced moments of elation and laughter, as well as moments of depression and tears. I have reached and stood upon some of the highest peaks on Earth, where practicing present-moment concentration has been so valuable for me. I have been privileged to attain the summit, both mentally and physically."

The fascinating woman practices more of her exercises as she continues, "Do you live in the present, or are you always rushing from one task to another, one patient to the next, looking to the future but harping on the past?"

Abigail explains the next set of exercises before replying, "I've never thought about it before. I guess, like everyone else, I rush from one thing to another, never stopping and taking in the moment."

*But didn't I live in the moment today?* Abigail thought, recalling her trip to work. Goosebumps run down her arms. *Why today, just before meeting this lady?* A stirring, new insight emerges from the back of her mind: *Become the student and learn from Mrs. Watkins. Let her guide you, and you will find clarity in your path.*

Time is a commodity that, once past, can never be reclaimed. Moments in time can never be changed or repeated. Abigail realizes, if she misses the opportunity to learn from this patient, she may never get another occasion like it. She is desperate for discernment and wisdom.

"I would love to learn how to fully live in the moment," she says. "I'm always eager to learn and gain insight and wisdom. To be honest, I am struggling with certain aspects of my new career path and personal life. I do feel I have been blessed and guided in an almost spiritual fashion, and I'm grateful for that, but I am unable to unleash my full potential. Please speak openly to me."

# Chapter 3

## A Call from the Burning Bush

After her exercises, the silver-haired lady asks, "Have you ever heard a voice directly instructing you to go on a quest into the unknown?" She settles back in the bed. She is now the Teacher.

Abigail leans forward in her chair and glances at the curtain around the bed. She feels it provides at least a little of the privacy the conversation deserves, but she knows the three other patients in the four-bed room will still be able to hear them.

Mrs. Watkins closes her eyes, allowing Abigail the opportunity to reflect on the question. The question makes her think deeply. It feels as if the past five years of her life have been just a voice, a clear, commanding voice, indeed calling her into the unknown; she realizes she would give up her security and comfort on hearing it. When it comes to explaining the voice, she cannot find the words she needs to evoke understanding; words evade her, and she believes no one will ever understand.

Lines crease Abigail's forehead, making her look older than her years. As she recalls a shameful experience, those thin lines move closer together into a frown:

*The world spins as she lies on the cold, hard tiles. This is a vasovagal syncope attack in full swing. The beating of her heart slows. The pressure in her arteries drops to the point where her cerebral cortex lacks the oxygen-rich blood it desperately needs to function. The brief loss of consciousness is surreal, and, although her body is in a state of momentary shock, she can feel the emotions which have caused her distress.*

She has kept these shameful emotions hidden, believing nobody will ever understand her anguish. Too brave for too long, she has wrapped the shame with layer after layer until no one can see the shame, while she slowly suffocates.

*She sweats as she lies on the cold tiles in the middle of Winter, a paradoxical response. Nausea hits and she pulls herself up. She fumbles through the low cupboard, looking for a bowl in case she needs it. She is still too dizzy to stand. She knows shame, a devastating emotion is the root of this incident.*

The voice she has heard so many times has called her to move forward but has never allowed her to settle down. Because of this voice calling her to an unknown goal, she has made many decisions that have been disruptive to her family. She trusts that eventually; she will feel a sense of fulfilment and contentment.

The talented Therapist had previously worked as a specialist in her field in a large, public hospital. Because of the logistical challenges of travelling to and from the hospital, she had convinced her husband to sell the home they owned free and clear; uproot their children and move closer to her place of work. It had been difficult to sell their home of 14 years. Her children had resented her for a short while when she took them away from their friends and enrolled them in a new school.

*The sweat beads roll softly down the side of her prominent cheekbones as she lies on the floor and replays the decisions she had made and the sacrifices her family had made to accommodate her.*

To live in this wonderful, newly-refurbished home, her dream home, they needed her salary to help cover a mortgage they weren't prepared for. Due to a weak property market and a squatter camp that was starting to move closer to the home they owned, they had to sell it at a lower price and had been unable to find a suitable house within the same price range.

After two years in her new position, despite improving her patient-handling skills and conflict management, which she had practiced daily at an intense level, she had lost touch with reality. She had spent more time at the hospital now that the drive home was shorter. Her closest friends and family members had tried to express their concerns about the change in her normally-bubbly personality. She knew they were right. She had changed. She was heading for burnout. The hard work and long hours had taken their toll on her; she had realized it was an unhealthy situation and affected her life on every level.

After an argument with a colleague at her former work site, her on-the-spot decision to resign had caused her immense shame. She was ashamed she had uprooted her family on what she felt was a whim in the first place, and now felt was all for nothing. She was ashamed she had put them in debt, which was not only reliant on her income but was a sum she would be unable to cover. Following the call of that voice had come at great cost.

*Teacher on the Mount*

Trouble at home had ensued, as she knew it would. Her shame had caused her to withdraw from her family, which frustrated her husband. All of a sudden, she had no job, and she felt her husband would never understand. She reached a low point, lower than any she had ever experienced. Feelings of loneliness and darkness became faithless companions.

What she had learned was that darkness and loneliness were fertile ground for starting to search for meaning. The smallest amount of meaning in the darkest moments can keep the flame of hope alive, she discovered. It was the loneliness that remained and rose to the surface to be dissected yet again.

"That's a very interesting question to ask," Abigail replies, bringing herself back to the present. "Yes, I have heard that voice. That is the voice I have been following for many years now, Mrs. Watkins, and I must confess that it hasn't been easy or comfortable to do what it has instructed me to do. The quest has, at times, left me with shame and in tears."

Mrs. Watkins uses pillows to prop herself up before she replies, "The guiding voice which calls people to a quest has been present for many years. Allow me to share this story with you so you may understand more easily.

"Thousands of years ago," she began, "a King was looking for a leader. The leader needed to be courageous, persistent, and obedient to the voice. You see, the King had lost his people to another nation, a nation that was stronger than his own.

Egypt, at that time, was not only a mighty nation that could overpower others with its army, but it was also a visionary nation. Egypt had needed slaves; the

*Teacher on the Mount*

slaves were required to carry heavy material and build the architectural designs envisioned by the Egyptians. The slaves had been taken from Israel, so it was the Israelites who were made to work their fingers to the bone. They were beaten by the Egyptian soldiers who made sure they didn't waste a single minute while working in the searing heat of the day. The Israelites had suffered. The King of the Israelites had endured enough; he heard the cries of his people and had seen their profound hardships.

The Israelites had been enslaved because of their lack of trust in their King. They had not heeded his voice. They had strayed. They had followed their own ways, and it had resulted in their enslavement by powerful Egypt. Although the King was deeply saddened and distressed for his people, he had been left helpless. The Israelites would not listen to his instructions. They needed a new leader who would free them from slavery, and to whom they would listen.

*"Who will hear the voice and accept the quest to help others?"* The King thought to himself. *It will have to be a man I can teach and send to the Israelites, a man who will be accepted as a leader.* The great King of Israel devised a plan.

"He had heard about a man who had been looking after his father-in-law's flock. The man was an Israelite but had been raised as an Egyptian."

Abigail interrupted, asking, "How did this man come to be raised by Egyptians when the Egyptians used the Israelites as slaves?"

Mrs. Watkins replied, "Pharaoh, the Egyptian king at that time, had decreed that all baby boys were to be thrown into the Nile River. He had been afraid one of them may become powerful enough to dethrone him. The man's mother, Jochebed, hid her baby son as long as she could until she no longer could.

"When the baby was three months old, she carefully made a basket from bulrushes, lined it with pitch and asphalt to waterproof it, and carefully put her baby in the basket. She placed the basket between the reeds in a river where she knew an Egyptian princess bathed."

"As the princess was bathing one day, she saw the basket in the reeds. She approached it and noticed the baby. He was warmly wrapped and seemed content. The princess couldn't resist. She picked him up, took him to her palace, and raised him as her own. He became royalty. He was educated well. The baby boy was named Moses because he was taken out of the water."

"But why would Moses leave the comfort and luxury of the palace?" Abigail asked, intrigued by this man who had seemingly gone from royalty to a shepherd.

"Moses's mother had told her other children about their brother Moses, and how he had become royalty." His sister had watched the Egyptian princess take baby Moses out of the river. Years later, Moses's siblings had been captured by Egyptian soldiers and made to work as slaves.

"One day, Moses took a walk to an area he had never visited before. He had never approved of the way the slaves were treated, and he had decided to see for himself how they were abused."

"As he passed a group of slaves, a girl spoke to him. She told him she was his sister and that he was an Israelite. Her words shocked him. He stared at her momentarily before dismissing her."

"His sister was upset. She had heeded the voice that had told her to speak up. She had expected something more from Moses. She had ignored the constant cautioning of her mother and siblings to keep quiet, and they feared she would be beaten, taken away, and killed as punishment for her disrespectful behavior towards the Egyptian prince. But she had unknowingly planted a seed by speaking the truth," said Mrs. Watkins, followed by a yawn. She stretches and swings her legs over the edge of the bed.

"I know you're tired, but please tell me what happened next!" exclaims Abigail.

"We are just getting started. I will certainly continue," the silver-haired lady responds. "I just need a glass of water."

"I'll get it for you," Abigail says, jumping from her chair. "Your knee will be a bit tender after the exercises, and you should rest it a bit afterwards." She picks up the jug from the bedside table, pours the ice-cold water into a glass, and hands it to the wise old Teacher. Mrs. Watkins empties the glass in a few deep gulps.

"Ah, so refreshing," Mrs. Watkins smiles. She enjoys the simple pleasures of life. Abigail wonders how this is still possible at her age when other patients of similar years lack enjoyment even from the most luxurious of items.

The Therapist places those thoughts to the back of her mind and takes her seat once again. She waits while Mrs. Watkins makes herself comfortable on the bed. She begins speaking.

"So, after his encounter with the slave-girl, Moses returned to the palace. The thought of what the slave-girl told him played on his mind. She had said he was an Israelite; she had said he was her brother." But how could that be true? He had a family and life here in the palace. He had always been Egyptian.

"Day after day, the words of the slave-girl haunted Moses, and he had found himself questioning his life. He had tried to speak to his mother, but she dismissed his questions. His mother's dismissal had fertilized the seed, and he had become sure she was lying to him." Perhaps, he thought, the slave-girl had spoken the truth.

"One scorching day, while Moses was walking past the slaves who were hard at work, he heard the crack of a whip. A cry of agony filled the air. He turned in the direction of the noise and saw an Egyptian soldier standing over a slave, a stream of fresh, red blood trickling down the slave's back. Moses's anger at the treatment of the slaves had grown since he had met the woman who claimed to be his sister."

"Moses shouted to the soldier, who was getting ready to strike again with more force, to stop, but he was too late. The whip landed another blow on the slave's already-bleeding back. The soldier raised the whip once more."

"Moses ran towards the soldier, who was not listening to him. Anger blinded him, and he lost touch with his royal manners and restraint. The soldier drew back in fear as Moses rushed towards him, rage twisting his features. Moses pushed the soldier off the scaffolding and to his death. Looks of disbelief were visible on the faces of the slaves. Nobody had ever stood up for them. "

"In shock and fear, Moses ran from Egypt and his life of royalty. Moses started a new life as an Israelite in a new country." He had found contentment.

"He met Miriam, an Israeli woman, fell in love, and later married her. He lived a simple life tending his father-in-law's flock. But he could not stop thinking about what he had done and about the people who were still enslaved in Egypt."

"The King of Israel approached Moses and his plan to make Moses the new leader was put in action."

"Moses had decided to look for a new feeding area for his father-in-law's flock. He led the flock to the back of the desert, to Horeb, where a mountain reaching as high as 2285 meters above sea level was visible. He left the flock to graze on the lush green grass in the shadow of the mountain."

"Exploring the area, Moses's attention fell on a burning bush. As he neared the bush, he noticed that the fire was not consuming the bush. He was curious to see why the fire did not consume the bush. He moved closer."

"As you know, dear Abigail, there are laws of nature on Earth. Think about the pulling force of gravity on our bodies. It is very constant, right? You would expect the fierce heat of the fire to obliterate a mere bush." So, Moses anticipated that the might and force of the flames would destroy the bush completely, as logic dictated.

"A vision appeared within the flames of the burning bush, causing Moses to jump back." A voice called

Moses by name; he was calmed by the voice and answered, saying, 'Here I am.'

"The voice warned him to not come closer to the burning bush. It told Moses to take off his sandals because he was standing on holy ground. "The voice assured Moses that He was the King of Moses' father and grandfather. Moses hid his face because he was afraid to look at the King.

"The King continued," Mrs. Watkins said, closing her eyes as she tried to recall the words as accurately as possible: "'*I have surely seen the oppression of My people who are in Egypt and have heard their cry because of their taskmasters, for I know their sorrows. So, I have come down to deliver them out of the hand of the Egyptians, and to bring them up from the land to a good and large land, to a land flowing with milk and honey, to the place of the Canaanites and the Hittites and the Amorites and the Perizzites and the Hivites and the Jebusites. Now therefore, behold the cry of the children of Israel has come to Me, and I have also seen the oppression with which the Egyptians oppress them. Come now, therefore, and I will send you to Pharaoh that you may bring My people, the children of Israel, out of Egypt.*'[1]

"Moses was amazed at what was playing out in front of his eyes." Lately, his days had been filled with peace, except for the constant concern for his siblings and fellow Israelites in Egypt. It was a comfort that the King wanted to deliver the Israelites from their slavery. But the King had wanted him to go and talk to Pharaoh, the man who had raised him in the Egyptian palace. Moses expressed his concern about having to

---

[1] Exodus 3:7-10 NKJV

face the ruler of Egypt, as well as to free the Israelites from their bonds. He was certain they would not trust a former Egyptian prince.

"Moses asked who he would say sent him?" The voice assured him that He would accompany him and, when they asked for the name of the person who had sent him, Moses should answer, '*I AM WHO I AM, and I AM has sent me to you.*'[2]

"The voice also promised Moses, '*I will certainly be with you. And this shall be a sign to you that I have sent you: When you have brought the people out of Egypt, you shall serve God on this mountain.*'[3] The King pointed to the mountain in Horeb. '*This is the reason for the mountain's name.*' The glowing heat experienced by Moses in his encounter with the burning bush was the reason the mountain was called Mount Horeb," Mrs. Watkins explains.

"You may ask the reasonable question: Why am I telling you this story, and is there a deeper meaning for your life?" She leans forward and waits patiently for an answer.

Abigail moves back in her comfortable hospital chair to think about the question posed to her.

There is so much she wants to know about this amazing story. Although she vaguely remembers a friend telling her the story of Moses, she has never heard the full story before.

A nurse enters the room and asks if she can have a few minutes with Mrs. Watkins to sign her discharge

---

[2] Exodus 3:14 NKJV

[3] Exodus 3:12 NKJV

papers and finalize the discharge process.

Mrs. Watkins says with a smile, "Give us 15 minutes and then join me here again. I'm excited to share more with you, dear." She shifts her attention to the nurse.

Abigail leaves the room, her head spinning. She considers all she has been told. She ponders the suffering of the Israelites and how the King wanted to rescue them from their slavery. She wonders about Moses taking off his sandals because he was standing on holy ground. She contemplates the quest Moses had been given, with only a promise to save his family and fellow Israelites, but with no immediate reward. She mulls over the burning bush, the vision, the King who called himself 'I AM WHO I AM' and the promise that Moses would service the King on top of the mountain.

# Chapter 4

# The Call to Help Others

"Welcome back, my dear Therapist Abigail," Mrs. Watkins says with a smile.

"Is everything set for your discharge?" Abigail asks.

"Almost," Mrs. Watkins replies.

"Let's run through the exercise regime once more then. We also need to make an appointment for you to join the next Osteoarthritis Support Group's exercise and education class. You will love the group. They are positive, full of energy, and have a true love of life," Abigail says.

She is amazed at how perfectly Mrs. Watkins carries out the exercise regime she had given her earlier that morning. She finds the vast amount of knowledge Mrs. Watkins has about pain management and exercises amazing. Abigail is used to assisting patients who know very little about exercise and often live a sedentary lifestyle. In most cases, they find exercise a chore rather than a way of life.

"How do you know so much about exercise principles and pain?" Abigail asks as she sits down.

"It is not only Moses who has experienced the exquisite beauty and unnerving silence of the harshest places on Earth. I have reached the peaks of spectacular high mountains. Why do you think my knees are worn out? I'll tell you about my mountaineering days a bit later though if we get a chance."

"I do hope we get the chance," Abigail replies. "For now, though, I have so many questions about the Moses story. The voice called Moses to a quest with the promise to save his family and fellow Israelites, but there was no clear instant reward for Moses, so why was Moses instructed to take on the challenge? Who is the King who calls himself 'I AM WHO I AM'? Why was serving the King on a mountaintop seen as a reward?"

Abigail stops to take a breath. She says with sadness, "I have the feeling I may have missed out on a lot in my childhood, Mrs. Watkins. My parents are wonderful people with good hearts, and always have the best intentions for me. However, they never read me stories like this, the story of Moses and the Israelites. Is it a well-known story?"

Mrs. Watkins replies, "My dear, don't be distressed or saddened. You will realize that your life, growth, and understanding are in accordance with the plan and purpose of your time on Earth. There is no one perfect plan which everyone must follow and achieve. Every plan is individualized. Let me explain and, at the same time, answer some of the burning questions you have about Moses.

"Let's start again from the beginning. Moses only heard the voice because his mother had obeyed the very same voice when he was a baby only three months old. Can you imagine how difficult it must have been for the mother to put her baby in a basket, to know that she would never hold him again, and to know that he would be brought up by another woman? The strength, obedience, and faith of Moses' mother were as sturdy as the hardest rock and as small as a mustard seed. After only 30 to 40 days from germination, the humble and small mustard seed grows into one of the largest plants."

Mrs. Watkins recites another piece she recalls from memory, "*'I say to you, if you have faith as a mustard seed, you will say to this mountain,* 'move from here to there,' *and it will move, and nothing will be impossible for you,'*"[4]

Abigail notices that Mrs. Watkins always closes her eyes when she recites something, as though digging into the deepest recesses of her mind to retrieve the important information.

"Where can I find the book where you found that piece on faith and the mustard seed?" Abigail asks.

"All in good time, dear. Allow me to continue. If Moses' mother had decided it was too big a sacrifice, Moses would have been put to death and would not have been able to save the Israelite slaves. Here, I have to say that we should be careful not to advocate giving away our new-born babies. Those were treacherous times. Moses was also under the watchful eye of his sister, who hid close to the river until the princess took him from the water.

"Obedience to the voice and acceptance of a dangerous and difficult quest was not only essential for Moses to live a life filled with purpose but also to help his fellow people. In this concept lies the first secret I want to share with you. When you hear that voice calling you to a quest that will be beneficial and uplifting to your fellow human beings, go for it! The voice will

---

[4] Matthew 17:20 NKJV

most likely come as a thought or a whisper that only you can hear. The fulfilment, joy, and contentment you receive after helping others will reward you on an emotional level which will affect your mental and physical wellbeing. It is true that in giving you will receive," Mrs. Watkins states.

This is the first transformational lesson the bright young Therapist learns.

Abigail rises and walks to the window. Looking out through the glass, she sees the iconic tower seen in pictures depicting the City of Gold, Johannesburg. The reflective thoughts come back into consciousness, and she decides to share them openly with her newly-found teacher.

"There have been moments when I could not tell whether I was accepting a quest because of what it will mean for others, or for my selfish reasons. I have been racking my brain and questioning my thoughts and actions. I have been unable to explain any of this to my husband, which has caused a divide between us. Although he respects my decisions and is always supportive, I know he often disapproves, because I cannot explain to him why I do what I do. Words have so often eluded me, and I'm left questioning the voice. That is why it is so invigorating to hear you speak about the voice of the King, calling Moses towards a quest to help others.

"Everything looks like it is stacked up against Moses, though. He will have to face the family who raised him and the family who essentially gave him away. Even the land to which he will lead the Israelites,[5] the

---

[5] Exodus 3:17 NKJV

land overflowing with milk and honey, had been occupied by many other tribes," says Abigail as she turns to face her teacher.

Mrs. Watkins pours herself another glass of water and takes a sip. "At first, it very often appears to be almost impossible," she says as she absentmindedly swirls the ice in the glass. "The quests that will benefit others require much sacrifice on the part of the person who accepts the responsibility and picks up the reins as the leader.

"Let's take the example of business owners. From day one, they make sacrifices as they build and then run their businesses. The first sacrifice made by any business owner is suppressing his or her ego, personal pride, and concern for self. They work long hours, often using their finances to start the business. They spend little time with their families and must live frugally, especially in the first few years when the business is in its infancy. A business owner's life is not always to be envied. For the owner who accepts the responsibility, if they can hang on, fight the right battles, let go of the petty matters, and have faith in the promise that they will reap rewards, it is all worth it. I can assure you of that! Building a business from the ground up, employing and shaping people and allowing them to grow, and having those employees remain loyal, despite anything, is a reward itself. Add to that the financial reward as the business grows because of these devoted and happy employees."

"Mrs. Watkins, I must tell you, I have heard the voice telling me to start a non-profit organization for disadvantaged scholars in South Africa who have learning and literacy challenges. The voice came in the form of a thought after I had a conversation with a fellow physical therapist who wanted to start a non-profit organization. It was the very first time I had heard about a non-profit, and I immediately started doing research. Could I also help my fellow South Africans to live a better life?

"Not even an hour after our conversation about non-profit organizations, a small, square booklet was delivered to our offices. The heading read something like 'Gauteng non-profit organization makes a difference.' I immediately sent my colleague a photo of the front page of the booklet. We were both astounded. I told her to start pursuing her dream and start the organization. She responded that it was not so easy, and the sacrifices would be too big. Now I understand fully what you mean about every leader having to make sacrifices for their quest. It requires strength and faith to follow the voice because the rewards are rarely instantaneous."

Abigail shares freely, her inhibitions melting away. Every minute spent with this amazing woman strengthens the bond she feels developing between them.

"What you are saying is exciting to hear; it shows your deep faith and inner strength," Mrs. Watkins says. "I assume you didn't only do the initial research on how to start a non-profit organization, but you have succeeded and you are now actively working in it?"

Abigail smiles and nods.

Mrs. Watkins continues, "With Moses, as with any leader, the sacrifices preceded the reward. Before Moses could lead the people to the Promised Land, he had to go back to the Egyptians and speak the instructed words of the King, win the trust of the Israelites, and show an enormous measure of trust, strength, and belief in the King.

"We so often make the mistake of thinking of sacrifices only in material terms. This is partly true. Often, it's sacrificing one's self, ego, and plans, to name but a few. The second transformational lesson is that a leader must sacrifice the old self, old ways, and be transformed within to be able to help other people long before the reward will be reaped.

"It goes hand in hand with the question you asked me earlier on: Why did the voice of the King appear in a burning bush? The four natural elements are water, air, earth, and fire. Fire has the immense power to ravage acres of grasslands and forests. Do you recall the fires blazing in the Amazon? The devastation of fires even rampaged through the breathtakingly beautiful Knysna forest. While the fire rages with fury, it spreads effortlessly and, despite all resources and manpower attempting to stop the spread, the fire remains difficult to control. It is not just the natural fire that is difficult to extinguish, my dear. It's even more impossible to douse the human spirit, once it has a goal, passion, and purpose in life.

"We will get back to this in good time. For now, don't take the burning bush in the literal sense. The King appeared to Moses in the burning bush to pique his curiosity, to see that this appearance is not ordinary but rather something very rare and exceptional. Moses' full attention was captured in an instant; the fire illuminated the power and glory of the King.

"Wisdom and knowledge are also indicative of fire in many cultures, and the King exemplified His knowledge by declaring how He was aware of the suffering and bondage of the Israelites. Wisdom was portrayed in the well-thought-out plan He created to save the Israelites with Moses' help.

"Moses went from receiving the education and living the lifestyle fit for a prince in a king's palace, to tending the sheep in a barren, thirsty land. Here, it is clear the King often works in ways that are not always clear at first but become beautiful as the plan evolves. I believe that the King appeared in the flames of the burning bush to show Moses that a new future awaited him and his fellow Israelites.

"After the intensity of fire, a diamond's purity is displayed. It is after the magnificent forests and woods have been burned down that the new grass and plants can grow. The old must die so the new can come forth. The King was acutely aware that, for Moses to become an inspirational leader to the Israelites, he had to undergo his transformation. This was achieved by the symbolic burning of the old Moses to allow the new transformational leader to accept his new call to duty," Mrs. Watkins finishes, as her cell phone rings.

Abigail politely leaves the room while Mrs. Watkins takes the call. The ward manager approaches her shyly. "I have been watching you all morning from my vantage point at the sisters' station. How is it possible that two people who have met for the very first time can talk for hours on end?" she asks politely.

To say that meeting and spending time listening to the wise teacher has been worthwhile for the young Therapist is an understatement. She manages to reply, "She is such an amazing, wise old woman. She shares her wisdom and knowledge freely. I have been listening to and learning from her all morning. There are times in life when you meet someone, and there is an instant bond. I have felt that with her."

"I must admit I felt the same when I talked with her this morning about her operation. How odd that she cancelled it because of a dream! Has she told you why?" the ward manager inquires.

"No. I am hoping it will come up, but I realize we are running out of time. I don't want this meeting to end Ward Manager," Abigail answers.

"I'm going on lunch shortly. Would you mind if I popped in and listened for a bit?" the ward manager asks.

"Of course not," Abigail replies. "I have the feeling our patient is willing to share her teachings with anyone willing to learn." Abigail hears Mrs. Watkins saying goodbye on the phone and re-enters the room.

"I am ever so grateful for your time, dear young one. You have graced me with your time and listened to an old woman's ramblings. Time is the most valuable commodity in this fast-paced, always-busy world we're living in. You have provided me with a home-exercise regime which I will do every day."

Mrs. Watkins smiles, but her smile fades as she continues, "That was my son on the phone. He has been called into an urgent meeting and will only be able to fetch me much later. I must try and find someone who is available. Oh, dear, I seem to be putting everybody out today."

"I will gladly take you home, Mrs. Watkins," Abigail says. "I still have so much I would like to discuss with you."

"Thank you, dear," Mrs. Watkins says, taking her hand.

The ward manager enters the room with a file in her hand. "I just need you to sign these papers, and you're free to go," she says. Mrs. Watkins chuckles as she signs the paperwork.

"I want to thank you, Ward Manager, for being so kind to me during my stay here. I know the trouble I have caused."

"Call me Sarah, please. Sarah Lee is my full name. It's always a pleasure to meet someone like yourself, ma'am. It is a rarity, and I feel very privileged," Sarah responds.

Mrs. Watkins takes her hand and squeezes it. "You are exceptional at your work. But I see deep despair in your eyes. I would still like to know your story. Your family, your history, your beliefs. Most importantly, your pain."

"How is it possible that you know of my sadness?" Sarah asks.

"Sit for a moment and tell me what you feel," Mrs. Watkins urges.

"I have been plagued with feelings of pain and grief. My baby died six months ago, due to an illness she was born with, and the pain I have been feeling since that day has been unbearable." Tears roll down Sarah's cheeks as if on a well-travelled path. "I only got to hold her briefly before she took her last breath. I have lost what I used to believe in. I have so much pain inside, and yet I feel so empty. I have asked people for advice, but nothing has helped. I don't know how to move on.

"Everybody tells me time heals all wounds. Does it really? I feel like nobody understands what it's like to lose a child. It's not fair. No parent should ever lose a child." The tears now fall freely as Sarah fishes a tissue from her pocket. She keeps a supply on hand at all times. Abigail can almost feel Sarah's pain emanating from her like Moses had felt the heat emanate from the burning bush.

Mrs. Watkins embraces Sarah and closes her eyes. She whispers words of prayer.

"I have something very special for you to read, but be warned: It's not easy reading," she says when her prayer is over. She scratches in her bag, pulls out a thin book and says, "Will you take this home with you, read it, and then come and visit me when you have a moment? We can sit down together and talk about the loss of your child. I can see that this loss hurts you to your core. I'm here for you."

Sarah takes the thin book Mrs. Watkins is holding out to her and whispers, "Thank you."

"You have my number on file," Mrs. Watkins says. "Please use it." Sarah hugs her goodbye and leaves the room.

"Let me help get your personal belongings together and take you home," says Abigail. Together, they leave the hospital and walk into the bright afternoon sun.

# Chapter 5

# Travelling Home

Leaving Mrs. Watkins at the entrance of the hospital, Abigail fetches her car. At the entrance, she jumps out and loads Mrs. Watkins's bags into the boot of the car. They both climb into the white Toyota's front seats. She enters Mrs. Watkins's address into Google maps. She presses the start button and waits briefly for the route to appear. It takes them west into unfamiliar territory.

She follows the instructions of the female voice advising her to drive 250 meters, then turns right. The surrounding buildings seem to loom over her from the western side of Johannesburg. They seem higher and somehow more menacing than what Abigail has experienced from the eastern side of Johannesburg. Her car moves between the skyscrapers she has only ever seen from a distance.

She glances at her passenger and smiles. She knows in her heart of hearts that Mrs. Watkins is the "real deal." *You seldom meet genuine people these days*, she thinks fondly. *In the course of just a few hours, a stranger has become a teacher and a friend.* And somehow, she knows the feeling is reciprocated.

"What do you do to pass the time in busy traffic?" Mrs. Watkins asks.

Abigail drops down a gear as the road begins to incline. "I use this time to improve my knowledge," she replies. "I spend most of the time listening to the material I download. Lately, my interest lies with research, in particular the distribution of data in statistics. I am struggling with the normal distribution concept, better known as the bell curve. I wish to use it in my postgraduate research study and share it with the students I will be supervising. Do you have any experience in the field of research and statistics?"

Mrs. Watkins leans back in the comfortable passenger seat and rests her head on the headrest. She folds her hands over her heart, closes her eyes, inhales deeply, and exhales slowly. Concentrating on her driving, Abigail maneuvers her little white car through the traffic-riddled city roads. Silence fills the space between the two females. Abigail, with her new awareness and sensitivity, chooses to let the silence continue; Mrs. Watkins must be deep in thought. At the red robot, the car comes to a standstill. Abigail turns to look at her silent passenger. It seems like an age since she asked her question.

The question about research and statistics must have triggered a memory for Mrs. Watkins. The raspy voice, when it speaks again, has a depth of emotion to it. "Oh, yes, I know much about research, my dear. I devoted twenty years of my career to research with my late husband. We used to spend hours talking about the similarities between the normal distribution bell curve and the mountain ranges we had climbed. We often made the analogy that research and life are like climbing a high mountain.

"At the beginning of life, our parents spend years raising us. For the child, the beginning of life is effortless, just like the beginning of a mountain climb, which starts with an easy hike. For some people, challenges arise from an early age; others only face challenges when they are older. The key point is that the ascent takes effort, courage, and resilience." Mrs. Watkins inhales deeply, sighs, and continues. "Research Mountaineers was the nickname our climbing companions gave us," she shares with a smile.

*A mountaineer AND a researcher, how amazing*, Abigail thinks to herself. She hopes to be able to spend much more time with this intriguing teacher, and extract as much wisdom as possible from her.

Abigail brakes slowly as they approach the back of a line of cars stopped at a red robot. She is acutely aware of how busy this area in Johannesburg is. People cross the road all around her, ignoring the pedestrian crossing in front of her. As she tries to watch everyone crossing the road, an uneasy feeling forms in the pit of her stomach. She has been blessed with intuition as sharp as the blade of a samurai sword, which she has learned to obey.

"We should get out of the city as soon as possible," she exclaims. The grey skyscrapers are suddenly pressing, almost suffocating her. She pulls her phone closer, wanting to view the virtual road ahead. She sees a red line indicating they have driven into a traffic jam in the heart of the City of Gold. She places the phone back in its familiar spot. *Unusual traffic for this time of day*, she ponders, *but hopefully we'll be out of it in a few minutes*. Taxi drivers clearly have the same frustration as they swerve between lanes and across intersections without waiting for the robot to change to green. *Deep breaths*, she reminds herself.

Cars start moving in front of her, clearing the road ahead for a few meters. The respite is short-lived. The robot turns red in front of her. Once more, she slowly pushes the brake pedal to the floor.

From the corner of her eye, she spots two young men approaching the car. The uneasiness she has been feeling erupts, and she knows something is not right. *It is not the kind of city you should ever feel calm and relaxed in*, she thinks. She instinctively removes the phone from its mounting and throws it on the floor.

On the other side of the robot, cars are piled up, as more drivers try to force their way from the right into the busy road. She watches as one of the men lifts his sweater with one hand and reaches down with the other. His hand emerges, holding a gun.

# Chapter 6

# Book in the Ward

Sarah has been an avid reader since childhood. Her love for beautifully well-thought-through and well-written books had her visiting every bookstore she came across. She often spent holidays meandering through streets filled with small shops in search of a book that piqued her interests. Old, dusty books used to make her eyes light up.

Used to. Since the death of her daughter, she has lost her passion for books. These days, she opens a book and, as soon as her mind starts relaxing, reality hits. Her mind wanders back to the daughter she will never hold again. With her mind unable to focus, she closes the book and puts it away for another day, a day she feels may never come.

The loss of her daughter has left her arms barren, and her heart shredded. *Can a heart that bleeds so profusely ever be mended?* she wonders.

With the book she received from Mrs. Watkins in hand, Sarah makes her way to the canteen. She sits down at an empty table in the corner, puts her book on the table, and takes her lunch out of her bag. The book is old and thin, but it has been well looked after. Perhaps the answers she so desperately needs are in this book.

She misses her daughter, dearly. Since that dreaded day in the hospital, she has turned her back on her beliefs. This act of rebellion frightens her, and she wonders about her daughter's soul. *What has happened to her soul if I no longer believe in Heaven? Is she safe? Did I doom her soul the day I turned my back on God?*

This gift must hold the key to the lock keeping her heart closed. She looks at the old, brown, leather-bound book. There is no title on the cover. She opens the book and starts reading:

*Joseph says: 'And why do you wonder that Jesus has risen? But it is wonderful that He has not risen alone, but that He has also raised many others of the dead who have appeared in Jerusalem to many. And if you do not know the others, Symeon at least, who received Jesus, and his two sons whom He has raised up – them at least you know. For we buried them not long ago; but now their tombs are seen open and empty, and they are alive, and dwelling in Arimathaea. They therefore sent men, and they found their tombs open and empty. Joseph says: Let us go to Arimathaea and find them.*[6]

"Another sermon," Sarah mumbles to herself. "Have I not heard enough of them from pastors, family, and acquaintances? As if it will make anything better or take the sting out of the hurt I'm in!" Anger builds up within her. She wants to scream what she has been thinking since her daughter died: *God has forsaken me!* Anger rises inside her every time someone talks about Jesus or God. *Where was He when I needed Him the most? Where was He when my daughter took her final breath? Where is He now?*

This struggle between God and the desolate Sarah

---

[6] Gospel of Nicodemus Part II, Chapter 1 (17)

started the second the doctors delivered dreaded news: There was little hope her daughter would survive. Every day since then, the struggle has escalated. Where was the God she loved and knew when her daughter needed healing? Why had He not healed the infant she had battled to conceive? Why had He left her, alone and emotionally crippled?

It was the faith her parents had taught her from a young age: Believe there is a higher being who had made her and placed her on this Earth with a unique and special purpose. She remembers that she was the reliable person, the one who was always there to help others through trauma, distress, and heartache. When they stood next to a grave, throwing gravel on the coffin of a loved one, Sarah was the rock people could count on, the steadfast prayer partner with love to give, and the proverbial shoulder to cry on. This has all changed.

She reads with tears in her eyes. One question bombards her thoughts: Why did the silver-haired lady give her a book of faith to read after Sarah told her she had lost her belief?

*Then rose up the chief priests Annas and Caiaphas, and Joseph, and Nicodemus, and Gamaliel, and others with them, and went away to Arimathaea, and found those who Joseph spoke of. They made prayer, therefore, and saluted each other. Then they came with them to Jerusalem, and brought them into the synagogue, and secured the doors, and placed in the midst of the old covenant of the Jews; and the chief priests said to them: We wish you to swear by the God of Israel and Adonai, and so that you tell the truth, how you have risen, and who has raised you from the dead.*[7]

Focus eludes this hard-working ward manager. Her mind wanders yet again to her daughter. The newborn lying in her arms was coughing. Moments after the caesarean birth, which the doctor had suggested because of Sarah's age, the pediatrician had given the baby oxygen. A strange bluish color had washed over the tiny miracle who had just taken her first breath. With her degree in nursing, Sarah knew enough to see when something was medically wrong with a patient. The imminent danger her new-born baby faced had been vividly clear. *Only the Lord God can save my precious daughter*, she remembers thinking. She had prayed constantly, prayers of healing, over her child.

She pulls herself back to reality and stares at the book she holds in her clammy hand. She continues reading.

*The men who had risen having heard this, made upon their faces the sign of the cross, and said to the chief priests: Give us paper and ink and pen. These therefore they brought. And sitting down, they wrote thus: O Lord Jesus Christ, the resurrection and the life of the world, grant us grace that we may give an account of Thy resurrection, and Thy miracles which Thou didst in Hades. We then were in Hades, with all who had fallen asleep since the beginning of the world. And at the hour of midnight there rose a light as if of the sun, and shone into these dark regions; and we were all lighted up, and saw each other. And straightway our father Abraham was united with the patriarchs and the prophets, and at the same time they were filled with joy, and said to each other: This*

---

[7] Gospel of Nicodemus Part II, Chapter 1 (17)

*light is from a great source of light. The prophet Hesaias, who was there present, said: This light is from the Father, and from the Son, and from the Holy Spirit; about whom I prophesied when yet alive, saying, The land of Zabulon, and the land of Nephthalim, the people that sat in darkness, have seen a great light.*

*Then there came into the midst another, an ascetic from the desert; and the patriarchs said to him: Who art thou? And he said: I am John, the last of the prophets, who made the path of the Son of God straight, and proclaimed to the people repentance for the remission of sins. And the Son of God came to me; and I, seeing Him a long way off, said to the people: Behold the Lamb of God, who taketh away the sins of the world. And with my hand I baptized Him in the river Jordan, and I saw like a dove also the Holy Spirit coming upon Him and I also heard the voice of God, even the Father, thus saying: This is my beloved Son, in whom I am well pleased. And on this account, He sent me also to you, to proclaim how the only begotten Son of God is coming here, that whosoever shall believe in Him shall be saved, and whosoever shall not believe in Him shall be condemned. On this account I say to you all, in order that when you see Him you all may adore Him, that now only is for you the time of repentance for having adored idols in the vain upper world, and for the sins you have committed, and that this is impossible at any other time.[8]*

It is true that Jesus Christ walked on the Earth and faced many challenges, much suffering, and persecution. From a young age, Sarah had sat in weekly

---

[8] Gospel of Nicodemus Part II, Chapter 2 (18)

Sunday school lessons, always right in front, wanting to learn more about the stories of old. The first man Adam and his companion Eve had been one of her most favorite stories until it came to the part where the snake craftily lured them to eat from the tree they were instructed not to touch. They picked the forbidden fruit and ate.

"The snake had achieved what he set out to do and had misled the first humans," her Sunday school teacher had said. "The first sin had been committed in the Garden of Eden. Adam and Eve's Creator had wanted so much more for them. He had wanted to keep them away from a sinful nature that He knew would take them away from Him. He had wanted mankind to love Him. He had wanted to love them and provide for their every need. The disappointment for the Creator must have been painful, and His anger towards the snake tremendous."

Miss Lisa, the Sunday school teacher, had possessed such a sincere and special way of teaching young children about faith, that the young Sarah could hardly wait for the next Sunday-school class, where she would listen to more stories from the book they called the Bible. Miss Lisa's favorite books in the Bible and the main themes she used to teach the children were about Jesus and His life on Earth. "Children, we can all learn how to live good lives when we study and follow how Jesus lived," she had said. This had made Sarah more excited to read the pieces which mentioned Jesus.

How long ago that feels and how unreal Miss Lisa's words seem, now that Sarah is in a world of pain. *I didn't read about Jesus losing a child, but He did lose his dear friend John.* She can't recall how He managed to continue His life and mission after the death of John. *Tonight, after my shift, I will go and read about John's death and the way Jesus coped afterwards*, she promises herself.

Walking back to her ward, Sarah feels changed. Her heart feels a little lighter. A shimmer of hope is present

# Chapter 7

## Trauma in the City

Why would this man have a gun? At this moment, the naivete of such a question quickly makes way for a rush of adrenaline, followed by what can only be described as divine intervention. Time takes on a different dimension; a split-second feel like minutes for the young mother of two beautiful and bright children.

She has heard of hijackings happening in South Africa, but she has never experienced one. In the world, there is probably no other city with more incidents of hijackings and trauma than right here where she finds herself. News bulletins on the radio and television give warnings of hijackings and attacks in the inner city of Johannesburg. Strangely, it makes sense. Had the news bulletins not explained that it happens daily? The only difference is that she never thought it could happen to her.

Thoughts flash through her mind. *Will this be our last moment alive? What if my children grow up without seeing their mother again? I haven't said goodbye to my husband.* Strangers walk up and down, passing the scene without noticing the imminent danger in which the two visitors to the city find themselves. Is this normal for the people living here? Do they ever notice?

With the gun now clearly visible, Abigail and Mrs. Watkins duck at the same time. Abigail surveys her surroundings once more before making her decision.

*Teacher on the Mount*

The pedestrian has disappeared for now. The congested traffic from the right has cleared as the cars ahead slowly move forward. Adrenaline pumping through her veins, she slams her foot on the accelerator. The Toyota Etios accelerates, causing a driver to toot viciously as she cuts that car off mid-turn. She quickly gains on the cars stopped ahead in the traffic jam.

Divine intervention opens a bus lane to the right. Abigail's foot keeps steady pressure on the accelerator, and she pulls into the open bus lane. The small Toyota jars them as it leaps over the five-centimeter-high concrete lane-divider. *Get distance between the car and the gun*, her mind screams. The incessant tooting and honking fade quickly as the little Toyota flee to safety. Only after passing the broken-down car causing the traffic jam does she move out of the bus lane back into the traffic lane. Without stopping, she drives on towards their destination.

Abigail breathes deeply in and out as a release from the adrenaline-filled action. She glances at her passenger. Mrs. Watkins looks understandably pale after their escape from the traumatic incident they just experienced, but there is a hint of a smile.

"My dear," Mrs. Watkins says as they leave the city, "you had a burning question about the King and Moses that I have not yet answered. Now is the perfect time to tell you who this King is. He is the divine protector and the protection we just experienced. The great 'I AM.' Have you ever heard of the saying, 'I am the alpha and the omega?'" As Mrs. Watkins asks the question, they crest yet another hill before descending sharply and levelling out on a smooth, open road. Abigail's mind becomes sharp and concentrated, the adrenaline having cleared her thoughts.

"I AM the alpha and omega. The beginning and the end. The King is the beginning and the end," Abigail states. "Did you notice that the curvature of the road we have just travelled on resembles the omega symbol?"

Mrs. Watkins smiles proudly at her student before replying, "It seems as though the traumatic incident we have just encountered has been beneficial to your understanding. It has opened your mind, and I hope it will allow your heart to also open. Allow me to explain, as well as give you the answer, to your last question about why a meeting on the mountain was given as a reward to Moses.

"When you look at the contours of the normal distribution curve in research statistics, as well as the curve of a mountain, if you use your imagination, you will notice a familiar pattern emerging. The pattern you find is the familiar omega symbol. At the bottom, we see a plateau before the ascent starts. The gradient becomes increasingly steeper and steeper. Much energy and endurance are required to continue the ascent until the highest peak is reached. The summit, the end destination, is particularly difficult to reach; very few people ever get to see the view from the summit. This is where the most beautiful photos are taken and where the battered and tired legs of mountaineers find rejuvenation. The mountaineers who set out on such a difficult journey, who make the sacrifices and pay the price, who put in all the hours of preparation, have the exclusive opportunity to taste the sweet victory of reaching the summit. The celebrations are huge. National flags are often planted on the highest peaks. They are members of a select few who get to see the world from this viewpoint.

"Moses was given the opportunity to take the journey the King set out before him. It was clear the journey to free the Israelites would not be easy. The Egyptians would fight and resist. The Israelites would question the trustworthiness of Moses. On his part, Moses had to commit to pay the price, trust the King, persevere in the face of danger, and not give up before he summited. The summit was, as promised by the King, eventually reached. Moses accepted the challenge of the climb and persevered until he tasted the sweet victory of the summit: an encounter with the King," Mrs. Watkins concludes as the car pulls in front of her gate.

For the first time, Abigail appreciates the blessing of inhaling and exhaling. She takes another deep breath: the first breath of a new life. A flood of emotion washes over her as she climbs out of the car to help Mrs. Watkins carry her luggage into her townhouse. "I need to go home to my husband and children Mrs. Watkins," says Abigail. "May I come and visit you?"

"Of course," Mrs. Watkins smiles.

After exchanging telephone numbers and a long hug, the new friends say farewell.

# Chapter 8

## John the Baptist's Death

Everyday life can be turned on its head in a split second. One moment it is excitement, anticipation, hope, love, fun, then comes the turning tide. People have tried to explain it with "different seasons of life," "ups and downs," or "Murphy's law." Pain has marred many lives and has pushed people to the ends of their wit, strength, and endurance. These moments of emerging hopelessness leave tears running down cheeks. Sarah knows this too well, as her thoughts wander back to her daughter's diagnosis in the neonatal unit.

The neonatal intensive care unit personnel had done all they could to try and save her baby's life. However, childhood interstitial lung disease, a rare disorder, was diagnosed too late and had already run its destructive, rampant course through the baby's immature lungs. Sarah watched as her child suffered from shortness of breath, fast breathing, low oxygen content in the blood, and low lung function. Her beautiful daughter was dying in front of her.

The doctors had explained that childhood interstitial lung disease was a group of possible and varied lung diagnoses. One specific diagnosis would be difficult to make. The disease damages the alveoli lining deep inside the lung. The alveoli or air sacs, responsible for the exchange of life-giving oxygen adversely affect the bronchial airway tubes that take oxygen into the lungs. No cure existed. Only a miracle could have saved her baby. Sarah had spent hours clinging to hope, praying for the miracle she believed would happen. God was good. Surely, He wouldn't bless her with the miracle of a baby they had tried so long to conceive, only to take the sweet, innocent infant away so soon after birth.

The repetitiveness of the flashback memories drains her. It is like a bad song playing incessantly in her mind, one she is unable to stop. The question that has given her hope enters the chaos of her mind: How did Jesus handle the ups and downs of life? Even more pertinent for her was: How did He cope with the death of a loved one?

Sarah relives the tale she was taught by her Sunday-school teacher.

The relationship between John and Jesus had started before their respective births. Elizabeth was pregnant with John when she met Mary, who was pregnant with Jesus. Elizabeth and Mary enjoyed each other's company and, as they interacted and talked, the unborn baby John had kicked with excitement and anticipation for the birth of Jesus. John had paved the way for Jesus by announcing His coming. That was John's life purpose.

John had faithfully lived up to preparing the way for the coming of Jesus, not only while in Elizabeth's womb but also in Hades. John's soul had a divine purpose that was instilled even before his birth. These two sons grew up like brothers. John had even baptized Jesus.

Then the unthinkable happened.

John had been a brutally honest person. He had

reprimanded Herod for divorcing his wife and unlawfully taking Herodias, the wife of his brother Philip. Herod had imprisoned John.

At Herod's birthday party, the daughter of Herodias danced, and her dancing pleased Herod greatly. In his drunkenness, he promised the young woman anything she requested. At the request of her mother, the daughter asked for the head of John the Baptist on a platter. Herod was appalled by this request, but he reluctantly agreed. He had John executed in prison.

The tragic news of John's execution, His friend and spiritual brother, was relayed to Jesus by the disciples. John, a humble man, and dear friend, had not merely stood up for his beliefs, but he had openly verbalized them. In the end, his ways had caused his death. Jesus had loved John and was devastated by the tragic news.

Jesus' reaction had been to seek solitude. He had wanted to walk to the peak of a mountain where He could grieve the loss of his brother alone.

Bombarded by the incessant memories of trauma has made solitude a concept that only brings more darkness. Solitude fuels the sorrow; she tries to avoid it at all costs.

Sarah remembers that Jesus had wanted to climb the mountain to be alone, but He had been denied the opportunity. A multitude of people had searched for Him and had found Him just as He was about to start His ascent. They had wanted to be in His presence, experience His company, and be under His teachings. They had wanted Jesus to heal them. Jesus had become known for these powerful gifts and feats.

His compassion for the multitude of people had

halted His climb to solitude to mourn the death of His beloved John. Although He had wanted to find the stillness and healing power solitude brings, He did not tell the people they were inconveniencing Him. They had left their homes and travelled great distances on foot to follow Him. Word had spread like wildfire, and soon everyone in the area knew about the miracles Jesus performed.

Jesus set aside his search for solitude to grieve the death of a dear friend, for it was His divine purpose to serve others, not to fulfil His own personal desires. The people needed Him.

Tears fill Sarah's weary eyes. Finding stillness in solitude was what He knew would bring the reflective opportunity to heal, but He could not do so, not at the cost of pushing people, albeit strangers, away. Regrettably, she pushed people away from her. Her actions have brought guilt. She had pushed away her ever-supportive husband and loving mother, the people closest to her. *Oh, how they wanted to hug and comfort me, and I did not allow them.* Tears flow down her cheeks once again. *Will I ever be able to stop crying?* she thinks.

After sobbing for what seems like hours, Sarah lifts her head off the soaked, rose-patterned pillow on her bed and walks to the bathroom. Through puffy eyes, she stares at her reflection in the mirror for the first time since her daughter's death. She cannot recognize the person she has become.

She washes her face with cool water and dries it on the soft, fluffy towel hanging on the rail next to the basin.

Feeling numb after the flood of emotions, she walks

*Teacher on the Mount*

to the kitchen and fills the kettle with water. As she waits for the water to boil, she looks out her kitchen window, over her rundown garden, and remembers how He had served the multitude.

He had performed miracles, He had cured people of illnesses, He had transformed lives for the better. The multitudes remained. Nobody returned to their villages for food, water, or rest.

The multitude had become hungry. The disciples had urged Jesus to send them to nearby villages to buy food. Jesus did not take their suggestion; instead, He instructed them to feed the people. He had known that some of the people would not make the journey. He had great concern for their safety. But the disciples had protested that there were many people to feed and very little food. Jesus had asked what food was available, and the disciples had produced five loaves of bread and two fish.

Jesus had taken the five loaves of bread and two fish, looked up to the heavens, blessed the food, gave thanks, and broke them into pieces. The disciples then began to distribute the food to the people present. Everyone had been fed sufficiently, and twelve baskets of leftover food were picked up.

Sarah, sitting next to her window, holds her cup of tea in both hands. At the same time, her thoughts shift between sadness, regret, John's death, and how Jesus was able to serve others during what was arguably one of the most challenging moments of His life.

*How did I lose the ability to serve others, where I used to be the person friends and family could rely on?* she asks herself. *I used to find so much fulfilment in helping others. Jesus was able to continue serving even though*

*He was distraught, with no resources at His disposal except what was present: five loaves of bread and two fish.* In the warmth of the morning sun streaming through the window, Sarah has finally found a moment of stillness and solitude. She takes out her old journal from the drawer of the coffee table.

Sarah carefully takes a pen in her hand and writes the date. Then,

*Dear Diary, how long has it been since I opened you and wrote something?*

The last date she had written was a few days before the birth of her daughter. The pages were filled with excitement and happiness. She remembers the chaos of the days preceding her caesarean as they did some last-minute shopping and made final touches in the nursery. She had closed the nursery door the day she returned home from the hospital. She had not crossed that threshold since.

Every word she writes seems to mend her broken heart just a fraction. Quite effortlessly, she fills the pages with her words. Without stopping, she writes about the death of her daughter. She writes about her regrets. She writes about the bitterness she has felt toward the Creator. She writes about how she has pushed away the people closest to her.

Her husband had left her because she wouldn't let him in. She realizes, despite her fear of isolation, she has unintentionally isolated herself. A deep loneliness descends. After pouring her heart out on the pages, she concludes with paragraphs devoted to what and how she wishes to change.

Jesus, on His ascent up the mountain to mourn the

loss of John, modelled the behavior she wants to display. He had neither shut out the disciples, nor the people who needed Him and sought His teaching. Instead of stillness and solitude, He had found the ability to teach and serve with a loving heart and a clear mind.

Sarah resolves to devote time daily to reading and writing. The first book she will finish reading is the book given to her by Mrs. Watkins, the book that has started transforming her.

# Chapter 9

## The Mentor

The grey-haired woman cannot help but feel relieved. Arriving back home after a traumatic drive through Johannesburg with the young Therapist reminds her of the comforts and peace her home brings to her.

Walking to her bedroom in the back of the small townhouse to unpack her bag, she notices the extent of her limp for the first time. Suddenly the short distance between the entrance and her bedroom feels farther than it should. The familiar sharp pain in her knee stops her momentarily.

She manages to enter her room and puts her suitcase on her bed. She moves aside the books she had received from her Mentor so many years ago and places her handbag in its accustomed place on the bedside table. She takes two red scatter pillows from the bed and puts them on the floor. Very slowly, feeling each sharp pain in her knee, she kneels on the pillows. She has grown accustomed to the pain during the years she has been waiting for the knee-replacement operation.

Her gaze moves upward to the bedroom ceiling while her wrinkled hands fold together in front of her chest. The expression lining her face is one of pain. She closes her eyes and breathes slowly and deeply. "May this bitter cup pass me by. Not my will but your will be done," she prays.

She pulls herself up, wincing as the pain sharpens. She sits on the edge of her bed and searches for a firm hold on the focus she has lost since her hospital visit. For a moment, she concentrates on her painful knee and the beating of her frail heart. She realizes she needs to turn her attention to the teachings of her Mentor.

"Join me on a trip around South Africa. I want to take you up my favorite mountains and show you the most breath-taking views," he had said to her one day while they were having lunch. It had been six months since he had started working in the department, and they had developed a fast and firm friendship.

He had caught her attention immediately. He was the epitome of tall, dark, and handsome. At just under 6-feet tall, the thirty-something towered above her, but he was in no way menacing. With his friendly brown eyes and charismatic personality, he was hard to ignore.

He had almost instantly picked up that she was finding the academic environment difficult and was struggling to cope with her research projects. The Mentor had been in academics for many years. He had opened the conversation around her difficulties with a few simple questions. She had found herself pouring out her heart to him, not only about her difficulties at work but also about her personal struggles.

The Mentor had emigrated from Jerusalem, where he had been appointed as senior lecturer at The Hebrew University of Jerusalem. He had exuded confidence and had displayed characteristics of kindness and helpfulness. He had often offended their colleagues with his straightforward manner and honesty.

The Mentor had always expressed his different, non-dualistic way of thinking about things.

Mrs. Watkins, at that time still young, already possessed an insatiable hunger to learn more and gain wisdom. She believed she could learn much from the Mentor.

"That sounds fantastic," she had exclaimed on hearing his invitation to explore South Africa.

With her knowledge of South Africa and his experience in mountaineering, they carefully planned a trip that promised to be scenic and memorable. They had selected relatively easy-grade mountains to start with, so she could gain experience. In those days, there were no fancy virtual lessons to eliminate the dangers of real-life experience.

The Mentor had taught her a lot before their departure. He had explained to her why it was vital to wear the correct attire during a climb. His first instruction to her had been to get proper footwear. She'd had to break in her hiking boots before the trip commenced.

The naïve young, Mrs. Watkins had followed his every instruction and had bought the best boots she could afford. The double-layered, pure leather exterior, rubber-soled boots had felt heavy, but they had been surprisingly comfortable. During the 100 kilometers she had had to walk before the trip to break in her boots, she had begun to understand her Mentor's advice that she wear two layers of socks with the boots. Her cotton socks caused painful blisters on pressure areas as she walked.

"It is best to get thick wool socks and thin nylon socks. Wear the wool socks over the nylon socks. This helps to keep your feet dry. Hiking trails and climbing terrain are frequently wet, and stream crossings are common," the Mentor had explained. "It doesn't mean your feet won't become wet and painful, but it will lessen the discomfort and help you endure the walk and continue hiking."

He had also explained having to walk kilometers with weights on her back, "We must carry 20 kilograms each, including food and equipment. You need to be able to balance the weight as you walk. Strengthening your body to be able to carry the weight will enable you to walk a few more kilometers and climb a few more feet before giving up. Endurance is built during preparation."

What the Mentor had taught her next had changed her whole outlook on life. He said, "I have walked the roads of Jerusalem and the nearby towns, and I have seen people give up too soon. There exists a lack of perseverance due to a lack of understanding. Life hands out different doses of struggles to each person. A lack of understanding and preparation leads to resentment and suffering."

The Mentor had handed her a maroon, leather-bound book. "Prepare yourself properly by reading this book. Use it as a study tool to write your thoughts and feelings after each section, and sculpt your reflection journal in this book," he had instructed. She had paged through the book and had found five double-sided white pages lined with gold after each section. "Follow these instructions, and you will not only reach your heart's desires and dreams, but you also will be able to weather any storm, be it personal or professional," the Mentor had continued.

"A strong heart and respiratory system are essential to a mountaineer. When the functioning of these organs is compromised, mountaineers are in serious danger. The respiratory system is often jeopardized on high-altitude climbs. The higher you climb, the less oxygen is available," the Mentor said. "A strong system will help you achieve great heights.

"The take-home message I want you to understand is that you need to challenge yourself by setting more demanding challenges, not only when it comes to climbing mountains, but also in your personal and professional capacity. You will experience many difficult environments and tough relationships in your life, just as you will experience many difficult terrains and natural elements on your climbs. To be able to handle the increasing demands, I want you to give it everything you've got, both mentally and physically. Always remember where you come from, so you remain truthful and righteous in every step you take."

Mrs. Watkins fondly remembers the passion the Mentor had shown while sharing his rich insights. He had always managed to transform his lesson in mountain climbing to a lesson she could apply to everyday life. His teaching style had shown compassion for the student and an unmistaken spirituality that made him genuine and trustworthy. It had often confused her as to why some of their colleagues were so violently opposed to his leadership and teaching style.

Mrs. Watkins reminisces on how quickly the first 307 kilometers had gone by, and how much she had enjoyed the intriguing conversations she had had with her Mentor.

*Teacher on the Mount*

Upon arriving in Clarens, they had made their way to their first overnight guesthouse.

# Chapter 10

## The Therapist and the Mountaineering YouTube™

After her ordeal of almost being high jacked, Abigail plans her route back home with extra consideration. She decides to travel east on the highway instead of taking the direct route through the inner city. The traumatized young women clicks on her preferred direction and presses start.

She minimizes the route display block and opens the YouTube™ app. Mrs. Watkins had given her a few keywords to look up. She chuckles as thumbnails of various YouTube™ videos fill her screen. The smiling face on some of the thumbnails is unmistakably the face of Mrs. Watkins.

During their drive to Mrs. Watkins's home, before the horrific ordeal, Abigail had expressed her dream of climbing the highest mountain in the world: Mount Everest.

"Passion and dedication to make it happen are your first steps to making your dream come true, my dear," Mrs. Watkins had said. "Search for YouTube™ videos. I will give you a list of keywords to help you find the best ones."

She had taken a pen and notepad out her bag, made some quick notes, and tore the page from the pad. She had folded the paper and placed it in the console between them. Abigail clicks on the first video before starting her journey home. The sweet voice of Mrs. Watkins fills the car.

"Exploring the highest peaks is not only an interest for mountaineers, but it is a competitive stage for many. Reaching the summit of Mount Everest, for example, allows the mountaineer to justly claim bragging rights. The mountaineer can plant his or her flag among the few flags that have been planted by previous mountaineers. Ambition drives ordinary people to put their lives on the line to achieve this goal.

"The 14 highest mountain peaks can be found in the Himalayas, and these peaks all rise over 8000 meters above sea level. China, India, Pakistan, Nepal, and Bhutan each have a share of this world-renowned mountain range. The mighty Himalayas have earned the respect of many mountaineers who have attempted to climb its highest peaks.

"The peaks are magnificent to observe from a distance or in pictures. However, mountaineers need to endure the harshest of climates. At these high altitudes, the air is devoid of oxygen, so the mountaineer is required to have oxygen tanks to get to the summit.

"Temperatures can drop from 20 degrees Celsius to between minus 20 and minus 60 degrees Celsius. It is difficult to comprehend the extremes. You cannot fully appreciate them until you find yourself within them. The higher a climber ascends, the lower the temperatures become. Conditions on the high mountains are tough enough under normal circumstances, but freezing, blinding blizzards make for an extremely challenging situation. A snowstorm accompanied by gale-force winds is treacherous. Temperatures well below freezing affect circulation to the skin. Frostbite is a real concern!

"It is, however, the unexpected which causes loss of life. No amount of planning or technique can prepare a mountaineer for the mighty avalanche. Mammoth pieces of ice situated high on these mountains can loosen suddenly. These ice pieces, with the help of gravity and the gradient of the mountain, start to shift. High forces cause these pieces to speed down the mountain. Human bodies are not made to withstand such forces. Soft and pliable skin, stretchable muscle and fascia layers, and strong bones covering vital organs and providing protection under normal circumstances are powerless against the devastating force of snow and ice.

"Adaptation is the key to survival. We spent weeks acclimatizing to the conditions and the altitude. We ascended from Base Camp to higher altitudes and then descended back to Base Camp, day after day. Adapt or die! Climbing these mountains is not for the fainthearted. Along with serious preparation and training, the mountaineer requires a patient mindset."

Abigail pulls into her driveway and feels overwhelming gratitude to be home safely. She envelops her husband and children tightly in the dawning realization that she is lucky to be with them again.

# Chapter 11

## The Manager and Hades

Sarah's thoughts reflect on her baby daughter.

She had sat next to her daughter's cot in the neonatal intensive care unit and wept. Her life was full in every aspect except motherhood. She had always loved children and had dreamt of having a couple of her own.

Sarah had put motherhood on hold for a while to build her career. Her plan had been simple. Build a career so that she could give her children the best of everything. She had decided that she would be ready for motherhood by the age of 35. They had had difficulty conceiving. After two years, countless doctor visits, and the eventual acceptance that the chances of them conceiving were minimal, they had begun the adoption process. A few months in, the miracle happened. She fell pregnant.

The hope, excitement, and gratitude she had felt over her daughter for those nine months had turned into a despair so crippling that she, like her newborn baby, could not breathe. Her beloved daughter would not have the chance of seeing her beautifully decorated room or feel the love of her mother's arms. The doctors had advised her that her infant's condition was too critical. To come so close to her dream, only to lose it, was too much for her to bear.

The traumatic memories of her child's death distract her from reading. She pulls her thoughts back to the book. With the thin, leather-covered book in hand, she settles in a comfortable garden chair. The Spring afternoon sun warms her skin as a cool breeze plays with her hair.

Her leave could not have come at a better time. She has set aside time daily for meditation, reading the book, researching historic texts, and writing in her journal. These have been instrumental in her healing journey. After just a couple of days, her heart already feels lighter and her mood more positive.

She has accepted that there is no timeframe for healing after a significant loss. She has learnt, however, that one should not stop serving others. Helping others helps you deal with your grief.

Knowing full well that mental health and psychology are not her areas of expertise, Sarah has come to understand she can't carry on destroying herself and pushing away the people closest to her.

Why did Mrs. Watkins give her this specific book? What else could this book possibly have in store? Curiosity grips her. Opening the book to where she had placed her bookmark, she continues reading.

*"While John, therefore, was thus teaching those in Hades, the first created and forefather Adam heard, and said to his son Seth: My son, I wish thee to tell the forefathers of the race of men and the prophets where I sent thee when it fell to my lot to die. And Seth said: Prophets and patriarchs, hear. When my father Adam, the first created, was about to fall once upon a time into death, he sent me to make entreaty to God very close by the gate of paradise, that He would guide me by an angel to the tree of compassion and that I might take oil and anoint my father,*

*and that he might rise up from his sickness: which thing, therefore, I also did.'*[9]

*It can be argued that the John referred to in the passage is not John the Baptist, but the description seems to fit. Is it even possible that, after passing on from this life into death, John was teaching in Hades? John had been a teacher to Adam, Seth, prophets, and patriarchs*, Sarah thinks deeply.

"This will take some time to sink in," she states.

She had spent time reading about the meaning of Hades and had come across a reference to the origin of the name, "Hades." It was derived from Greek mythology. The Greeks understood Hades as the abode of the dead and the god who rules this abode.

Her concern for her daughter didn't end on that tragic day when the tiny infant died. Quite the contrary. Her concern for her daughter has grown increasingly stronger ever since, and this growing concern has been torturous. Sarah has asked many questions about death and what happens after death. She has received no clear-cut answers.

"Your daughter is in Heaven, safe in the arms of the Savior," she remembers being told. But how can she be sure? *Death and Hades seem to be dark and scary for me. What would it be like for an infant?"* she wonders.

John, Seth, Adam, prophets, and patriarchs: some saints and many sinners in the same location, Hades and not Heaven. There is something fundamentally different in this explanation of life after death,

---

[9] Gospel of Nicodemus Part II, Chapter 3 (19)

compared to sermons she has heard.

"When you live a good life and know God and Jesus, Heaven will be your home after death. If you do not believe in God and Jesus or live a predominantly sinful life, then Hell is the destination after death," Sarah recites. This explanation has been preached to her from an early age.

Adam had not only been the first man on Earth, but he is known to have been the first sinner. Adam and Eve had been cast out of the Garden of Eden and separated from the presence of the Creator. Adam had gone to Hades, as did John, the faithful friend of Jesus and the man who stood for truth and righteousness. It wasn't only John, but also the prophets, patriarchs, Adam, and Seth. There is little doubt the prophets lived good lives on Earth. If anyone deserved to enter Heaven, it would surely be the prophets. But they did not. They had also been sent to Hades. One place, one abode after death.

The next intriguing concept from the passage is that John was teaching in Hades. One thing she can undoubtedly say is that, after death, the body remains on Earth. Sarah remembers her tiny, lifeless baby daughter lying in her arms. She held the little body for hours before handing her to the medical personnel. She vividly recalls the small coffin descending into the grave.

It must be the inner spirit of each person who has died which requires teaching and guidance. Was that what John was doing? Still, teaching even after death for the curiosity and craving of souls? "Oh, how relieved I will be if this is true. I can move on if I know my daughter's soul can still receive the teachings and instructions from saints like John, the prophets, and the remorseful, repentant first man Adam," Sarah utters pensively.

As she has so often practiced, she breathes slowly and rhythmically. Breathing deeply and intentionally has become a habit, resulting in mental stillness and healing. Another thought comes to mind. *If John, Adam, Seth, and the prophets have shed their Earthly bodies after death, how do they still know and distinguish each person?* 'I wish thee to tell the forefathers of the race of men.'[10] Only one race, the race of men. There is no judgement of physical appearance, race, gender, sexual orientation, or religion amongst the inhabitants of Hades. There seems to be more to life after death than what Sarah thought!

Her eyes move back to the pages that are opening wounds. Every passage of this book, if read carefully, not only opens the broken heart but brings the difficult questions to the fore, the questions that people are most often too fearful to ask. What happens after death? The questions and answers that this thin leather-bound book gives her a deal with human mortality. For the first time in a long time, something makes sense to Sarah. She knows her daughter's soul is alive after death. The knowledge of this helps her find answers and heal.

She continues to read.

*"And after the prayer an angel of the Lord came, and said to me: What, Seth, dost thou ask? Dost thou ask oil which raiseth up the sick, or the tree from which this oil flows, on account of the sickness of thy father? This is not to be found now. Go, therefore, and tell thy*

---

[10] Gospel of Nicodemus Part II, Chapter 3 (19)

*father, that after the accomplishing of five thousand five hundred years from the creation of the world, thou shall come into the earth the only begotten Son of God, being made man;*

*"'Does your father Adam want a temporary cure in the form of oil to cure his illness or does he want to experience healing from the source from which eternal healing originates,' the angel asked Seth. This teaching from the angel was of great value for all who heard it. The only begotten Son comes to give more than the oil that Adam is asking for. The Son, a physician of more than human physiology, but even the deep everlasting soul of man, will bring healing power over sin. He knows the root cause of the illness, not only the symptoms and knows exactly how to cure it.*

*"and He shall anoint him with this oil, and shall raise him; and shall wash clean, with water and with the Holy Spirit, both him and those out of him, and then shall he be healed of every disease; but now this is impossible. When the patriarchs and the prophets heard these words, they rejoiced greatly."*[11]

Sarah takes a sip of sweet tea and sits back in her chair to ponder what she just read. Adam had known he had a sickness. He had requested his son, Seth, to ask God, via an angel, to allow him access to the tree of compassion. From the tree, he could tap oil that may give relief from the sickness by lifting him.

Sickness is not an uncommon occurrence and has been part of her day-to-day life for the past sixteen years. She has tended to many sick patients during her

---

[11] Gospel of Nicodemus Part II, Chapter 3 (19)

career. She has taken care of many terminally ill patients. She has controlled their excruciating pain with medication to make their final days as comfortable as possible. Simple things can make a world of difference. A pillow can help a patient fall asleep if placed correctly to relieve pressure around a hip, shoulder, or sacrum. Terminal illness, ceasing life, is difficult for the patient, but the family and friends are who have to deal with the aftermath, as she experienced the day her daughter took her last assisted breath.

"Adam, however, was already in Hades, the place one can only be after death," Sarah says, putting her teacup on the garden table. "His sickness was then not a physical sickness but a sickness he experienced in another dimension, a dimension of the soul. Sin! Adam's sickness was a sin."

The angel who came to Seth after prayer had given him very insightful advice. To Seth's surprise, the healing power that was yet to come through the Son would not only have been for Adam's sin, but for the sin of everyone present in Hades. All the inhabitants in Hades had been under the sickness and yoke of sin.

Sarah knows little about oil as a healing agent. She opens her cell phone and enters search words in the browser. A list of references appears, and she reads.

From the earliest days in the Jewish culture, oil formed an integral part of their day-to-day existence. Israel and its climate were conducive to the growth of olive trees. Agriculture during the lives of ancient Israelites revolved around two months in a year when olives were picked from the trees, as per the Gezer calendar. Olives provided a vital source of plant fats in the diet of Israelites. Massive limestone presses crushed the washed olives in a basin. The olive mash was then placed into pressing vats. A weight that fit in the vat pressed the olive mash to squeeze out liquid. At this point, the liquid was not yet oil; it needed to separate. The result was glorious olive oil which was scooped off the top and placed in vats.

Olive oil was used as fuel for lamps to illuminate the darkness and provide light; it was rubbed into the scalp and limbs to improve cosmesis; it was used in consecrated meal offerings; it was used in the anointing of the priests, High Priests, and temple artefacts to make them holy; and it was also included in a medicinal mixture to heal wounds.

After reading and studying the significance of olive oil for the Israelites, Sarah understands why Adam had asked for oil. It was a very precious commodity used to anoint and make a person holy. The angel had given Seth a foretaste of the Son's healing.

Anointing with oil would be followed by rising out of Hades. Sin would be removed through washing with water and the spirit, which is needed to clean the soul. Every disease would be healed when the Son healed.

*Perhaps Mrs. Watkins gave me this book because she knew I also require oil to heal my sickness, just like Adam*? she ponders. She exits her browser, places her bookmark between the pages, and closes the book. As a chill taint the late afternoon air, she shivers and makes her way back inside.

She takes the piece of paper with Mrs. Watkins's telephone number out of her bag. "I will call her tomorrow," she says, placing the paper on the table and putting the book on top of it.

# Chapter 12

## Manager and Joseph

In the cozy townhouse, the midday warmth brings comfort to Mrs. Watkins's old, weary body. She is grateful that the townhouse is small. The bathroom, kitchen, living room, and bedroom are within a few yards of each other. The short distances are a relief when the pain in her knee twinges. She limps back to her bedroom, a cup of tea in her hands. The pain is a great reminder to do the home-based exercise program the young Therapist, Abigail prescribed to strengthen the muscles of the knee.

She climbs on her bed, sitting up against the headboard, and starts with the first exercise. After repeating the first two sets of the quadriceps-strengthening exercise, she moves into position for the next set of exercises. The ring of her cell phone startles her. She slowly swings her legs off the edge of the bed and answers the phone.

"Good afternoon, Mrs. Watkins." She immediately recognizes the ward manager Sarah Lee's voice and notices a difference. The young woman's voice seems lighter, somehow. "It's the ward manager from the hospital. I'm phoning to find out how you're doing."

"Sarah, it's so good to hear your voice, and what a surprise, too. I'm well, thank you. I want to hear how you are. How is your reading going?"

The valuable book she had given Sarah is filled with

life-changing insights that each reader must discover for themselves. She had gained immeasurable personal value from it.

Her Mentor had given her only one instruction along with the book: "After you have read, studied, and reflected on the content thoroughly, pass it on. Carry it with you everywhere you go. The person who needs the book will appear in your life; the hidden lessons you will learn from it will make you wise enough to know who the person is."

"Mrs. Watkins, before I get to that, I want to thank you for noticing the pain and sorrow in my heart and soul. I have been longing for some respite, and this book is truly giving me that opportunity. I haven't been able to stop reading. Although it is opening painful wounds, it has already provided the healing balm I have needed to soothe some of the pain. I have only read about a quarter of the book. There are some fascinating but equally difficult messages hidden in the text that I have to reflect on. I would love to get your insights. You did warn me that the book is not light reading," Sarah laughs. "The content has to be reflected on in moments of stillness. I have even found that writing has helped me to figure out how the content and secret mysteries apply to me personally."

Mrs. Watkins grins. She had hoped the life-changing book would find its rightful next owner. She opens the drawer of her bedside table, takes out a piece of paper, and ticks off the third-last item on the list. *My final to-do list*, she thinks.

"My dear Sarah, the pain that filled your eyes, although you tried to hide it behind your professionalism, was clear for me to see. I have felt that kind of pain. The pain of losing a loved one does not only change how our eyes look to the outside world but also it changes our view of and behavior in the world. Pain causes us to withdraw from our family and friends. It makes us cautious about taking future risks. Pain becomes visible in the eyes, the windows to the heart. That is how I could see you are suffering. I'm sure our paths crossed for a reason. I believe you needed that book before the pain derailed you. I hope the book will help you not only find your life purpose but also achieve it."

"I wish I could express how grateful I am, Mrs. Watkins. I know I am now on the right path, not only to recovery but also to find that purpose," Sarah says.

"I want to share a story with you that I believe will help you understand why it feels as if you're ascending a mountain in your journey to healing," Mrs. Watkins says. "The story is about a boy named Joseph, but it is a long story. Perhaps we should make a plan to meet instead."

"No, Mrs. Watkins, I think this story will be prudent for my situation and learning. Share your wisdom with me. Please share the story of Joseph with me," Sarah implores.

Mrs. Watkins begins, "Jacob and Rachel, with their children, lived in the Hebron Valley in Canaan. In his old age, Jacob had received the gift of two more sons, Joseph and then Benjamin. Although they were Rachel's first two children, they were Jacob's eleventh and twelfth. For a reason unknown to us, Joseph was favored by his father, and Jacob did not hide the fact that he favored Joseph; this enraged the older sons. You can only imagine how much jealousy would be caused when one is favored among so many.

"Jacob gave Joseph a highly-sought-after gift, a tunic coat made from the finest materials of that time and dyed with multiple bright colors. It was while Joseph was wearing this precious gift that he approached his family to tell them about two curious dreams he had dreamt the night before. The first dream was, according to Joseph's words: *'There we were, binding sheaves in the field. Then behold, my sheave arose and also stood upright; and indeed, your sheaves stood all around and bowed down to my sheaf.'*[12] The second dream, according to Joseph's words, played out like this: *'Look, I have dreamed another dream. And this time, the sun, the moon, and the eleven stars bowed down to me.'*[13]

"Well, you can imagine how greatly this infuriated Joseph's brothers; the dreams fueled the fires of their jealousy. After hearing the second dream, Jacob also rebuked Joseph; he couldn't believe the arrogance of his young son. The notion that Jacob and Rachel would bow to Joseph was preposterous.

"The older brothers conspired to kill their arrogant younger brother," Mrs. Watkins says, pausing to sip her tea.

"What happened then?" asks Sarah.

"Are you up for a story game while I tell the rest of Joseph's story?"

"Yes, absolutely," Sarah answers.

---

[12] Genesis 37:7a
[13] Genesis 37:9

"During the rest of the story, whenever you hear that Joseph was unfairly treated, or when he was blessed, I want you to ask, 'and then?' There is a life lesson hidden in this for you. Are you ready?"

"Let's do this!" Sarah voices her eagerness to start. Mrs. Watkins hears her excitement and smiles at the chance to teach Sarah another life lesson.

Mrs. Watkins takes another sip of her tea and makes herself comfortable on the bed.

She continues, "Life back then revolved around agriculture, tending to sheep in the pastures, and producing food for their survival in the land. Jacob protected his two youngest sons and only sent the older brothers to tend to the flock in the fields of Shechem. One day, when the older brothers were out in the fields, Jacob called Joseph to him and told him to go and see if his older brothers were doing well. Joseph wanted to please his father and obeyed the instruction. He packed some food and set out on his long journey from the Hebron Valley to Shechem. He was unaware of what would be waiting for him on the other side of the valley."

"And then?" Sarah interjects quickly.

"You are good at this," Mrs. Watkins chuckles. "The geography of Hebron Valley and its surrounding areas are mainly up-and-down trekking terrain, with mountains reaching heights of almost 1400 feet. The Dolomites and hard Eocene chalk lined Joseph's trek to Shechem. It was an effort to reach his brothers."

"And then?"

"Joseph followed information from bystanders and

found his brothers in Doran. His brothers watched him approach; he was unmistakable in the multicolored tunic he wore. 'Here comes the dreamer,' they mocked."

"And then?"

"Their plan involved killing him and throwing his body in a pit."

"And then?"

"Instead, his brothers sold him as a slave. They contrived a lie and ripped his multicolored tunic, presenting the shreds to Jacob as evidence that Joseph had been killed by wild animals.

"Unfortunately, I must get going," Mrs. Watkins says. "I have much business to attend to today. I quickly want to tell you how you can use the story of Joseph for a positive change in your life.

"What Joseph was learning was, in fact, a lesson in mastery of how to apply the 'and then' concept, just like you have practiced. The kind of mastery I'm referring to is the ability to have emotional control amidst opposition, mastery in your life perspectives and thoughts, and to speak kindness and truth amidst heartache. To remain unaffected by exterior circumstances and the behavior of negative people can only be achieved through the internal mastery of oneself when life deals a blow. The product that the hard work of self-mastery will bring is utmost control of thoughts, spoken words, and eventually, actions.

"The lesson involves climbing a proverbial mountain. The mountain each person must climb is a different and unique life purpose. To reach your purpose, you must climb your mountain. For some people, the mountain they must climb is a mountain of tragedy. It all starts by taking the climb, just as Joseph did."

Sarah asks, "Mrs. Watkins, what do you mean? Joseph walked over a mountain, straight into the hands of his malicious brothers, and into danger."

"We are taught we will remain safe if we stay where we are if we never take risks," Mrs. Watkins replies. "It is the opposite when it comes to self-mastery and overcoming the bitterness of life. It takes courage and faith to take the journey. To climb the mountain of tragedy and stare a traumatic event in the face is as tough as climbing the very highest mountains on Earth. People who refuse to climb the mountain become blamers, often vengeful, bitter, and regretful of not making the climb.

"Dear Sarah," Mrs. Watkins asks, "would it be possible for you to meet with me on Saturday? I know a quaint little coffee shop around the corner that serves the best coffee."

"Yes, please. That would be lovely," Sarah replies.

"Continue to read the book, and we can discuss your thoughts and insights," Mrs. Watkins instructs.

They finalize the arrangements for the meeting and say their goodbyes. For the first time since her dream and meeting Sarah and Abigail, Mrs. Watkins feels a pang of sadness at the limited time she has left.

# Chapter 13

## Mentor Teaches on Road trips

Clarens is situated centrally in South Africa. It is an artists' retreat, loved for its solitude and beautiful, surrounding mountains. The fresh air, open skies, and hospitality of the friendly people living in Clarens made it a perfect start to their journey.

The tar road had changed to a gravel road as they journeyed to Aspen, the guesthouse situated at the foot of the Clarens Mountain. Their hostess had welcomed them with a hearty "Welcome to Aspen. I hope you will enjoy your stay."

"Thank you. We are excited to be in your beautiful town," the Mentor had replied.

After unpacking their bags in their designated rooms, they had set off to dinner. After enjoying a scrumptious prawn and chicken curry, the student asked the question she had wanted to ask the Mentor for a long time, "How do you stay so level-headed, non-judgmental, and honest at the office, amidst the fierce opposition you are getting?"

This the Mentor had answered without hesitation, "I get opposition everywhere, but I know it's not a personal attack. Dualistic thinking has ruled cultures, institutions, religious communities, and societies for centuries. This knowledge has helped me realize it's not always a personal attack. You learn to pick up if a person has a dualistic perspective and thinking by the way a person speaks and acts. They try to make you feel as though they are right, and you are wrong. It creates inequalities and feelings of superiority. They will make judgmental statements on race, gender, religion, class, culture, or sexual orientation. They categorize everything into little boxes and don't approve of anything that doesn't fit. People who have a dualistic perspective follow what is accepted by the majority. They don't step into the unknown, nor express their own views when their views differ from the masses.

"Teachers who are dualistic thinkers believe every question has only one right answer and they are the ones with that right answer," the Mentor continued. "In relationships, dualistic thinking can create division between people, because the dualistic thinker believes he or she is always right and is not open to any other views that may be presented. Although they follow the most commonly-held beliefs of a group, they still feel isolated and alone, because they create division between themselves and others.

"Dualistic thinkers display characteristics of egocentrism. They are very emotionally reactive and often say things without thinking. They are self-preoccupied, rigid in their views, and judgmental. Their train of thought loops continuously: right or wrong, good or bad, beautiful or ugly, like or dislike, love or hate, holy or sinful. It is all black and white; there is no in-between. Sadly, the lives of dualistic thinkers become centered on condemnation, fear, and judgements.

"The wise words of Jetsunma Tenzin Palmo say it all: *'dualistic thinking disconnects us. Once we recognize the nature of the mind it's compared to the sky because you cannot cut it into pieces. It's what connects us all. Non-dualistic thinking leads to truthful words, words become impactful actions, actions will lead to consistent and healthy habits, habits become your character, and a great character will determine your destiny.'*"[14]

Mrs. Watkins had listened intently as the Mentor spoke with passion and conviction.

He continued, "We are taught dualistic thinking from an early age by our family and friends. They don't do it intentionally. Most dualistic thinkers don't realize they have judgmental opinions, emotions, and beliefs. It's just how they've always been.

"They plant the seed in their children, and the weed grows as the children grow. Their fertilization is society at large, but fertilization is not always needed for the growth of this weed. Fertilization only makes it grow quicker and stronger.

"Knowing this information has helped me to not judge, not speak negatively, nor act harshly towards the opposition and negativity from people. I spend quiet moments in prayer and work relentlessly on what I believe to be my life's purpose. I try and help others to achieve non-dualistic thinking.

"I use parables or stories, if you will to teach non-dualistic thinking to everyone, I'm fortunate to meet if they will listen. With my students, we start class with five to ten minutes of stillness during which we search for these deep-seated, unhealthy beliefs, which we acknowledge by writing them in a journal. I then share parables, which allow alteration of the unhealthy patterns of thinking and actions. This helps my students

---

[14] Quotation by Jetsunma Tenzin Palmo

know that the mind and body are not separate and isolated, but rather, they are interconnected. This is why stillness of body and writing of thoughts help with the shift from dualism to non-dualism. I have received such heart-warming emails and letters of gratitude from students for this teaching.

"A non-dualistic view means that circumstances and ideas should be questioned or challenged. Peace of mind that a non-dualistic view brings is valued higher than judgmental thoughts and feelings. So, the best gift you can give yourself is letting go of what you think you know. Successfully doing this will allow your mind the freedom to explore unknown territory," the Mentor concluded, before paying the bill.

"I miss the presence of the Mentor," Mrs. Watkins laments as her thoughts move from the lesson about becoming a non-dualistic thinker to the beautiful hikes, they had taken in the Golden Gate National Park.

The knowledge the Mentor shared with her during their road trip was unforgettable. Traversing the Drakensberg was followed by a trip to Lesotho, where they visited a ski resort. The Afriski Resort, situated in the Maluti Mountains, is one of only two ski resorts in southern Africa. It was during their visit to the resort that she had realized just how good the Mentor's mountaineering skills were.

The Mentor and she, wearing those broken-in hiking boots, had practiced walking on the icy slopes with crampons, as well as stopping techniques, after slipping on a mountain slope. It was clear the Mentor had climbed many mountains. His vast experience and passion for mountains were clear by the way he had taught her and the enthusiasm with which he shared his knowledge.

Her heart had broken after their trip. He had announced he would be unable to join her on other trips. He said, "I have taught you everything you need to know. It is time I move on. There are still many out there who need my assistance and guidance."

He had encouraged her to pay it forward. He instructed her to teach others in a non-dualistic way, to share with others what he had shared with her. Although he left her after that, she knew he would always be close.

As the busyness of life took over, her promise to her Mentor slipped to the back of her mind. She had taught non-dualistic thinking; she had paid it forward, but she had never made it an active purpose in her life. Her dream in the hospital was a reminder of her promise; her dream had given her the awareness to assist the two lost souls who were put in her path.

# Chapter 14

## Everest Mountaineering Clothing and Equipment

The crackling of a fire and the sound of two young children joyfully playing close by relaxes Abigail. She has learnt to savor this time with her family. Before her, the African sun sets, the sky aglow with bright shades of red and orange. Nothing beats the sight of an African sunset.

Tonight, dinner is cooking over a wood fire, on the metal-drum braai built by her tall, blue-eyed husband. She held his hand and lay her head on his shoulder as they watched the children play in the garden. Abigail felt her heart swell with love for her family.

"You will not believe the day I had," she says, as her husband stands up to tend the fire. "I met a patient who, after waiting for many years for a knee replacement, cancelled her operation this morning. She is such an amazing person, and we talked for hours. Due to her unexpected discharge from the hospital, her son was unable to fetch her, so I took her home."

Trying to keep her tone matter-of-fact, she adds, "We got caught in an awful traffic jam. We were almost highjacked."

"What? I can't believe what I am hearing. Are you ok?" her husband exclaims, the color draining from his face as he turns to face her.

"It was scary," Abigail admits, "but it felt like we were protected. Everything seemed to fall into place to allow us to escape unharmed. Mrs. Watkins remained calm throughout the entire ordeal! She is so wise about life.

While the meat finished cooking on the braai, Abigail continued talking about the events of the day with her husband who was clearly concerned and grateful to have his wife safely home. After the meat was cooked a perfect medium-well done, they carried the meat indoors where the children joined for dinner. Sitting at the round, wooden dining room table, Abigail shares with their children all about the fascinating patient, Mrs. Watkins, whom she met in the hospital. Together the Grace family eats their dinner with intermittent discussions around the highest mountains on earth, how people are pushing the human barriers in mountaineering, and what equipment and skill are needed to successfully and safely climb at high altitude.

"Mrs. Watkins was a mountaineer and a researcher years ago. She has given me resources to help me learn about preparing to climb Mount Everest," Abigail utters with excitement in her voice. "Come and watch one of her videos with me," she continues while picking up her cell phone and finding the next video.

Abigail's video screen opens; Mrs. Watkins's voice begins: "For a Spring expedition to Everest, every mountaineer needs to have the correct gear. You should have the following gear before setting off. Although I am providing you with a list, please talk to a seasoned mountaineer who can assist you with your choices of gear in the current market.

"Make sure your priorities are right before starting your shopping trip. You don't need the most expensive equipment and clothing on the market, but you will want to spend more on some things than on others. Look out for specials and buy the best you can with the money you have available.

"Let's start with footwear. You will encounter different terrain on the expedition. Firstly, for the approach trek, a pair of well-fitting, waterproof hiking boots are recommended. As you approach Advanced Base Camp, you'll need to don a pair of durable and warm hiking boots. I can't express enough about how essential it will be to find the correct hiking boots, and how important it is to buy footwear of good quality. Purchasing cheap boots that are wrong for the terrain could place you in life-threatening situations. Best-case scenario: Cheap boots will cause painful, blistered feet.

"Your hiking boots should be lightweight and comfortable, offering ample ankle support. If the boots require custom-fitting features, such as a piece of Velcro to avoid the boot's tongue moving laterally, ask a reputable mountaineering clothing shop well in advance to make these alterations.

"You will need to pack a second pair of boots for the actual climb from Advanced Base Camp and higher, where you will encounter the waterfall and icy, steeper ascents. These boots should have more ankle support for the rougher terrain and for traversing icy slopes.

"These boots are waterproof. The laces are hidden on the inside, with a waterproof gator-zip system on the outside, which keeps out the snow and water. They are also warmer and have a double-insulated layer and an inner booty. The inner booty can be removed for even more warmth. If you feel the need, during the final ascent to the Everest summit, you can use electronic foot warmers. These are inserted into the boots and are heated by a battery-powered controller strapped to your torso that will enable you to put the foot warmers on and off.

"The soles of the climbing boots are slightly thinner to allow for more flexibility while climbing. The soles have toe wells at the front and heel wells at the back, which make them compatible for crampon systems. You must ensure you have boots which are crampon compatible.

"Semi-automatic crampons are fixed to the boots with a plastic strap at the front of the boot and a plastic clip that clips into the heel well at the back of the boots. A strap is wrapped around the boot to secure the crampon in place.

"There is a wide variety of boots for you to consider," Mrs. Watkins says, then images of boots fill the screen, followed by different types of socks.

"You will need a variety of socks, all made from moisture-wicking materials to keep your feet dry. You can put some socks over a light-wicking, wool baselayer. These socks keep your boots dry, which is essential, as you will be wearing your boots daily with no time for them to dry out, particularly in the colder temperatures as you climb higher.

"Socks made with merino wool or bamboo fibers are comfortable. Longer socks are good to prevent chafing from your hiking boots. Ski socks can help avoid chafing from the toe seam.

"Lightweight tracksuit pants and thin, long-sleeve shirts are ideal for the start of the trek. These should be sun-resistant, wind-resistant, and breathable.

"As you climb higher and the temperature drops, you will need to start adding layers. Your base layer should include materials that are breathable, durable, and lightweight. Silk long-johns and vests are a good choice. Ensure your clothing, especially the clothing closest to your skin, is made from moisture-wicking material insofar as you can. Although the temperatures drop, the walking and warm clothing may cause sweating. You need to ensure the moisture is kept away from your skin.

"Merino-wool shirts are comfortable and lightweight and work well over the vest. A fleece layer keeps the core temperature of the body comfortably warm. You should also pack a waterproof down jacket. Add layers as needed.

"Shell pants fare well against mountain abuse. The pants are made from synthetic fabrics that are resistant to abrasions and tears. Softshell pants are water-resistant and protect you against light rain and snow. They are not, however, waterproof, but they do dry quickly when they get wet. Hard-shell pants are made from a tightly-woven face-fabric. These pants are waterproof and breathable and are often lighter and more packable than softshell pants.

"Gloves are important to protect your hands. Start with a pair of fingerless gloves, such as fishing gloves, which allow for dexterity. These gloves will protect your hands against possible abrasions if you slip, without making your hands hot and sweaty. As the temperatures drop, you will need thick, warm gloves to prevent frostbite. Hand warmers can be inserted into the gloves as you climb. Summit mittens are a must.

"At the start of your trek, wear a comfortable, sun-proof cap with a neck gaiter. A sweatband comes in handy. Buffs are also useful in many situations. A buff is lightweight, breathable, wind-resistant and moisture-wicking because it is made from 100% microfiber polyester. It can be worn around your neck, or your head, ears, or mouth to either absorb moisture or provide a buffer against dust and cold. As you climb higher, a warm, lined hat will be a necessity. Make sure your hat won't interfere with the use of your oxygen mask. Ensure you also pack a helmet for safety.

"You want to minimize as much skin exposure as possible, not only from the cold but from the sun and dust, as well.

"Now for the essential equipment: An emergency blanket serves a dual purpose. In the case of an emergency, you can use it to keep you or a climbing friend warm. Having it close to the top is useful for this reason. You can also use it as a groundcover to put your tent on.

"Pack your clothing compactly in a trash bag to keep it all together. You will also be carrying food, water filter, tent poles, water bottles, emergency first aid kit, sunglasses, sunscreen, toiletries, batteries, a tent, and the sleeping bag. Ensure you pack as light as possible. On the outside of your rucksack, have your crampons, ice axe, picket, and shovel.

"Pack your harness rack close to the top when the route requires climbing. A harness is a must-have piece of gear on which you carry cord for the prusik, chest harness, webbing for your runners, the personal anchor, and rope. The hardware you need will include a rescue pulley, ice blade, and carabiners. A compass is a useful tool. Although only a few are required in your group, it's always best to have too many than none at all."

# Chapter 15

## Darkness in Hades

The first rays of early morning light shine through the drawn curtains of Sarah's bedroom. She has had a good night's rest, the first one in a very long time. She stretches as she sits up. She makes herself a cup of tea and climbs back into the warm comfort of her bed.

She takes her the book from the bedside table and opens it to her bookmark. She moves her journal and pen to within easy reach on the table for when she wants to write down her thoughts while reading this fascinating book.

*And when all were in such joy, came Satan the heir of darkness, and said to Hades: O all-devouring and insatiable, hear my words. There is of the race of the Jews one named Jesus, calling himself Son of God; and being a man, by our working with them the Jews have crucified him: and now when he is dead, be ready that we may secure him here. For I know that he is a man, and I heard him also saying, My soul is exceedingly sorrowful, even unto death. He has also done me many evils when living with mortals in the upper world. For wherever he found my servants, he persecuted them; and whatever men I made crooked, blind, lame, lepers, or any such thing, by a single word he healed them; and many whom I had got ready to be buried, even these through a single word he brought to life again.*[15]

Sarah lays the book on her bed, lifts her journal and pen, and begins writing:

*In this passage, the heir of darkness, Satan, is worried and goes to Hades. Here Satan approaches him and starts by sugar-coating the words all-devouring and insatiable.' Satan clearly knows Hades, and I wonder why Satan has fostered a relationship with Hades. Perhaps referring back to his fall as an Angel when he had been close to God and in communion with his fellow Angels? Once referred to as Lucifer, the most beautiful of all the Angels in heaven, a musician of note, he had rebelled and sinned against God. Sin referred to also as disambiguation is where Lucifer transgressed against the divine laws set out by God for the Angels and where he became so corrupt that it spilt over where he wanted to cause others to also sin. The corrupt thinking and actions are seen even after his fall in what is written in this passage where he said, 'by our working with them the Jews have crucified him.' The wicked and destructive acts of Satan caused other humans to fall from divine, heavenly providence and God's grace. It must have been a fierce rebellion, and assuredly Lucifer wanted to be more and ultimately the most powerful. He was cast out of heaven.*

Sarah places her pen down next to the passage she has just written and sits back in her chair, thinking deeply about the opposites that exist in life. Left versus right, up and down, light and darkness, and the often unseen but ever-present good versus evil. Sarah

---

[15] Gospel of Nicodemus Part II, Chapter 4 (20)

has always been fascinated by the opposites that color in human existence. It is only now while reading the book that she begins to understand how the intrinsically connected opposites are. Light only resulted because of darkness. There would be no need for light if darkness did not precede it. Night makes way for the day. If there was no good, no evil would have existed. Sarah is reminded of a poem she adores that describes the opposites perfectly. Standing up from the chair, she walks over to a bookshelf in her living room for the book titled Paradise Lost written by the 17th century English poet John Milton.

Sarah picks up the book, turns the pages to John Milton, who has written about another opposite, Heaven and Hell, and reads.

*'Paradise Lost by John Milton, 1667*

*Say first, for Heav'n hides nothing from thy view*

*Nor the deep Tract of Hell, say first what cause*

*Mov'd our Grand Parents in that happy State,*

*Favour'd of Heav'n so highly, to fall off*

*From thir Creator, and transgress His will*

*For one restraint, Lords of the World besides?*

*Who first seduc'd them to that foul revolt?*

*Th' infernal Serpent; he it was, whose guile*

*Stird up with Envy and Revenge, deceiv'd*

*The Mother of Mankind, what time his Pride*

*Had cast him out from Heav'n, with all his Host*

*Of Rebel Angels, by whose aid aspiring*

*Teacher on the Mount*

*To set himself in Glory above his Peers,*
*He trusted to have equal'd the most High,*
*If he oppos'd; and with ambitious aim*
*Against the Throne and Monarchy of God*
*Rais'd impious War in Heav'n and Battel proud*
*With vain attempt. Him the Almighty Power*
*Hurld headlong flaming from th' Ethereal Skie*
*With hideous ruine and combustion down*
*To bottomless perdition, there to dwell*
*In Adamantine Chains and penal Fire,*
*Who durst defie th' Omnipotent to Arms.*
*Nine times the Space that measures Day and Night*
*To mortal men, he with his horrid crew*
*Lay vanquisht, rowling I the fiery Gulfe*
*Confounded though immortal: But his doom*
*Reserv'd him to more wrath; for now the thought*
*Both of lost happiness and lasting pain*
*Torments him; round he throuws his baleful eyes*
*That witness'd huge affliction and dismay*
*Mixt with obdurate pride and stedfast hate:*
*At once as far as Angels kenn he views*
*The dismal Situation waste and wilde,*
*A Dungeon horrible, on all sides round*
*As one great Furnace flam'd, yet from those flames*
*No light, but rather darkness visible*

*Teacher on the Mount*

*Serv'd onely to discover sights of woe,*
*Regions of sorrow, doleful shades, where peace*
*And rest can never dwell, hope never comes*
*That comes to all; but torture without end*
*Still urges, and a fiery Deluge, fed*
*With ever-burning Sulphur unconsum'd:*
*Such place Eternal Justice had prepar'd*
*For those rebellious, here thir prison ordained*
*In utter darkness, and thir portion set*
*As far remov'd from God and light of Heav'n*
*As from the Center thrice to th'utmost Pole.*
*O how unlike the place from whence they fell!*
*There the companions of his fall, o'rewhelm'd*
*With Floods and Whirlwinds of tempestuous fire,*
*He soon discerns, and weltring by his side*
*One next himself in power, and next in crime,*
*Long after known in Palestine, and nam'd*
*Beelzebub. To whom th' Arch-Enemy,*
*And thence in Heav'n call'd Satan, with bold words*
*Breaking the horrid silence thus began.*

After reading the poem, Sarah lifts her pen once more:

It is undoubtedly true that Satan works to corrupt others, just as he has corrupted fellow Angels and the Jews. Amidst the dark, sorrowful state He finds himself in, He wishes to steal the joy human beings experience on Earth and in Hades. Is it possible that when we are feeling joy, Satan comes to tempt us the most? Joy has become for me one of the difficult emotions to allow myself to feel. After losing my daughter, joy has been uncommon and when I feel joy, even for just a moment, it feels unfamiliar and wrong, wrapped in guilt. As in the passage I have just read, it seems that the experience of joy provokes Satan into action to attempt to cease the joy. Is it then not in the experience of joy that I can find healing? Is allowing myself the emotion and the experiences which bring about joy not the answer to my battle with grief?

The Son of God, while on Earth, also felt all human emotions and therefore Satan approaches Hades with the request to take hold of Him and bind Him. Jesus was exceedingly sorrowful and even went further in anguish. He exclaimed that He is sorrowful even unto death. To make a statement of the immense nature indicates that He suffered. The human experience is marred with moments of suffering. However, the only possible cure to the sorrow that suffering brings is easing into the moments in life that brings a measure of joy!

Hades says: '*And is this man so powerful as to do such things by a single word? Or if he is so, canst thou withstand him? It seems to me that if he be so no-one will be able to withstand him. And if thou sayest that thou didst hear him dreading death, he said this mocking thee, and laughing, wishing to seize thee with the strong hand: and woe, woe to thee, to all eternity!'*[16]

Hades, in this passage, considers what Satan is saying and the request to bind Jesus. Hades immediately sees what is going on and what the truth is. From the beginning of time, lies had been Satan's weapon with which he deceived and still deceives humans. Satan detests the truth because of what truth reminds him of. Indeed, Satan will not conquer. In the end, what is good will overcome what is evil. Satan will burn in everlasting fire. The battle from the beginning of mankind, for this reason, is a battle to win souls, that which Jesus and the King hold the dearest.

Sarah puts her journal aside and continues reading.

Satan says*: O all devouring and insatiable Hades, art thou so afraid at hearing of our common enemy? I was not afraid of him, but worked in the Jews, and they crucified him, and gave him also to drink gall with vinegar. Make ready, then, in order that you may lay fast hold of him when he comes.*

Hades answered*: Heir of darkness, son of destruction, devil, thou hast just now told me that many whom thou hadst made ready to be buried, be brought to life again by a single word. And if he has delivered others from the tomb, how and with what power shall he be laid hold of by us? For I not long ago swallowed down one dead, Lazarus by name; and not long after, one of the living by a single word dragged him up by force out of my bowels: and I think that it was he of whom thou*

---

[16] Gospel of Nicodemus Part II, Chapter 4 (20)

*speakest. If, therefore, we receive him here, I am afraid lest perchance we be in danger even about the rest. For, lo, all those that I have swallowed from eternity I perceive to be in commotion, and I am pained in my belly. And the snatching away of Lazarus beforehand seems to me to be no good sign: for not like a dead body, but like an eagle, he flew out of me; for so suddenly did the earth throw him out. Wherefore also I adjure even thee, for thy benefit and for mine, not to bring him here; for I think that he is coming here to raise all the dead. And this I tell thee: by the darkness in which we live, if thou bring him here, not one of the dead will be left behind in it to me.*[17]

*While Satan and Hades were thus speaking to each other, there was a great voice like thunder, saying: Lift up your gates, O ye rulers; and be ye lifted up, ye everlasting gates; and the King of glory shall come in. When Hades heard, he said to Satan: Go forth, if thou art able, and withstand him. Satan therefore went forth to the outside. Then Hades says to his demons: Secure well and strongly the gates of brass and the bars of iron, and attend to my bolts, and stand in order, and see to everything; for if he comes in here, woe will seize us.'*[18]

---

[17] Gospel of Nicodemus Part II, Chapter 4 (20)
[18] Gospel of Nicodemus Part II, Chapter 5 (21)

# Chapter 16

## Final List

Mrs. Watkins leans back in the chair positioned by the window. The afternoon sun heats her back. She unfolds the piece of paper she holds in her hands.

The dream she had had the night before her planned knee replacement made it crystal clear that she was not long for this world. She had immediately started her final to-do list.

"I don't have much time left to pay it forward as the Mentor had asked me to," she says mournfully.

She starts reading the list, which had grown, and ticks off the things she has already completed.

She ticks off: *give the book to a person in suffering*, and fondly thinks of Sarah. She adds, *help guide the suffering person to find peace*. She places a small P next to the item, knowing Sarah still needs further guidance. This item is still in progress.

The next item on the list is: *share the teachings of the Mentor*. She places a small P next to this item too, knowing she is working on it with Abigail.

She folds the paper again, stands up, and puts the piece of paper that contains her final to-do list back in her bag.

# Chapter 17

## Reaching your Everest

The drive to the Coffee Bean, the coffee shop around the corner from Mrs. Watkins's townhouse, was filled with talk of day-to-day life. The trip was too short for deep conversation.

Mrs. Watkins's request to meet had sounded urgent, so Abigail gladly makes the 45-minute drive from her house to fetch her. She knows she would do anything for the woman who is imparting decades of wisdom to her and showing her a new path in life.

Greeting customers and staff alike has become routine after several meetings with Mrs. Watkins. Abigail realized at their first meeting that Mrs. Watkins was well-known and well-liked in her community. They make their way to the back of the coffee shop and sit in their usual private booth in the corner.

"Tell me, my dear Abigail, have you finished watching the YouTube clips about what is needed to climb Everest?" Mrs. Watkins inquires after they placed their order.

"I have. You give so much value to your audience by sharing advice on what clothing, gear, and skills are essential before setting out on a mountaineering trip. Do you think I will one day be ready to take on the highest mountain?" Abigail asks. She lifts her cup to her nose and breathes in the rich scent of the freshly brewed coffee before taking a sip.

*Teacher on the Mount*

"Climbing Mount Everest requires top physical fitness," Mrs. Watkins responds. "You need climbing experience, exposure to high-altitude climbs, and mountaineering skills. There are different climbing techniques you will need to master for different environments. Mountaineering, free climbing, ice and mixed climbing skills, and aid climbing, which are all graded according to different scales. Here is a list of trusted companies and their contact numbers. I have used many of them myself. Call them and start building your competency. They are all close to Gauteng and will teach you all the skills you will need to climb different terrains. They can also put you in touch with reputable mountaineering groups you can join. They work with beginner climbers and will help ready you for your Everest climb."

Mrs. Watkins then takes a sketchpad and colored pencils out of her handbag and places them on the table. She asks, "Have you ever heard of a vision board?"

"I think we did one in school, but that was so long ago," Abigail replies.

"A vision board is a visual tool that allows you to map out your dreams and goals. It is believed that looking at it daily strengthens your resolve to reach those dreams and goals. The dreams and goals are embedded in your mind. Everything you do, even subconsciously, leads you to achieve those dreams and goals.

"To reach a goal as high as Mount Everest, you not only need technical expertise and experience, but you also need to be able to visualize it. Now, I want you to draw a map, similar to a vision board, of how you are going to achieve your goal. Use vibrant colors."

Abigail looks at her teacher in amazement. From

the moment she met this intriguing woman, she knew she was different from any person she had ever met. This strategy to draw a picture, add words to it, and color it rekindles her childlike love for nature and mountains. Abigail takes the sketchpad and places it in front of her. Reaching out to find suitable colors, she draws the brown route towards base camp, which then gives way to sheets of ice. Her hand moves upwards on the paper, drawing the ever-increasing ascent up the slopes of the illustrious mountain, culminating at the peak. Here she writes her name, draws a flag in the bright colors of her beloved South Africa, and writes "29,029 ft. on 16 May 2019." On the left of the page, she uses all her favorite colors and writes, 'I will become a master at practicing the following attributes: discipline, problem-solving, determination, patience, persistence, and grit. This will allow me to reach my own Everest'.

Abigail sits back, looks at her newly-created colorful dream map, and smiles. She has attempted difficult challenges up to this point and, although those challenges will be nothing like reaching Mount Everest, they have tested her persistence, discipline, determination, and fitness levels. An intense feeling of sharing some of her own experiences with Mrs. Watkins moves her to speak.

"This reminds me of the day I ran my fourth Comrades Marathon in 2014. It was a chilly Sunday at 5:00 am, and all the athletes were lined up for a grueling 89-kilometre run from Pietermaritzburg to Durban. I lined up with 14,693 runners, all of us excited and nervous. The normal starting procedures were followed: The South African National Anthem was played, followed by the theme music from *Chariots of*

*Fire.* With tears running down our faces, we awaited the starter's gun. We were off! We ran in initial darkness through the city of Pietermaritzburg towards the first obstacle of the day, Poly Shorts, a climb that warmed up the legs and took us up to Ashburton. Harrison Flats welcomed us and sent us on our way toward Inchanga, a hill big enough to cause some introspection of 'Why I am doing this race?'

"On Inchanga, and a few kilometers from the official halfway mark at Drummond, the realization struck me: I am not prepared for Comrades! I was panting because of the humidity, or perhaps it was just the reality of the demanding Comrades Marathon route that was staring me in the face. I had to regain some form of inward composure. Walking up the steep climbs, the tar hot under the soles of my shoes, past Drummond, I reached for my cell phone, wanting to call Lauren, my friend who lives on the route and the person picking me up at the finish line in Durban. I wanted to give up and quit the race. Participating in many running and cycling endurance events, I have come to know myself in a deep sense. I never allow myself to think of the people I love until the last ten kilometers, and only then do I allow tears of gratitude to flow and heal. At this moment, I was thinking of my loved ones at 45 kilometers. This was too soon!

"Thinking of giving up is a new concept for me. I've had to work hard and fight for every school grade and sports team. Personal victories always came at a high price. I continued walking uphill, my cell phone now back in my pocket! Now, Botha's Hill. From the corner of my eye, I saw a spectator with a beer in his hand and instinctively moved closer to him. 'May I please have a sip of your beer?' I asked. He reached into his cooler-box and pulled out a new beer, saying, 'Here you go; a new one for the road ahead.'

"It was manna from heaven for a tired runner, a runner at her wit's end. Drinking this gift, even though I don't enjoy beer, gave the necessary nutrients. After finishing half the can, I placed it strategically next to the road for the next runner who may need a sip of beer. A few minutes later, a large group of runners, fondly known as a bus, passed. Joining them helped me reach the last 17 kilometers. I finished the Comrades with a few minutes to spare.

"The victory was not my position or even the medal, it was for knowing that the incessant praying throughout the day and the loving grace of our Creator made it possible. He placed people on the route to encourage, supply, and share the road. For this reason, the race lived up to its name: Comrades! Even in the moments where I felt down, I persisted and never gave up! It was there on the long road from Pietermaritzburg to Durban that I had my very first experience of faith, where I felt the closeness of the Creator. I started believing and felt the calmness and closeness while being physically tested to the very ends of my own abilities and physical endurance."

Mrs. Watkins starts talking with a remarkable passion and conviction. Abigail has not yet experienced teaching of this magnitude and she listens intently.

"You will be ready to climb the highest physical mountains when you have made the effort to climb the invisible mountains that stand between you and the purpose you were created to achieve. My Mentor, the Son of the Creator and King, had loved climbing the highest physical mountains He could find. He used to climb them in search of solitude and closeness to his Father, the King, whom He had missed dearly. It had been on the pinnacles of these mountains where He had learned what his true-life purpose was. Although He had known His life purpose and had tried to prepare well for the final mountain ascent, nothing could have prepared Him for the daunting challenge he had to face while climbing the most difficult and painful mountain. My Mentor taught me much about how to face the extremely difficult climbs, and I will now share two of His mountains climbing experiences with you."

Mrs. Watkins takes a book out her handbag, opens it at the place where a bookmark in the form of a cross is marking the place and starts reading from it, "**Look the Lord your God has set the land before you; go up and possess it, as the Lord God of your fathers has spoken to you; do not fear or be discouraged.**"

"Let me tell you the story of the Mentor and the journey he had to face for his mountain climb," Mrs. Watkins says after they place another coffee order.

"As you know, the King has always longed for all human souls to commune with Him and has always worked through human beings to save the souls of those who fall into Satan's traps. Evil incarnate runs through Satan's being. He had once been so close to the King. His desire for ultimate power had caused his fall. Satan ruthlessly searches for the weakness in every soul and then tempts them to move them away from what he had once experienced – closeness to the King.

"Directly after receiving the holy baptism, the Holy Spirit had come upon the Mentor and His spirit was lifted. It had strengthened him but it had also led him into the desert. Receiving a special gift is worth nothing if it is not tested and used to help other human beings. The Mentor had known this well and had followed the promptings of the Spirit. For forty days and forty nights, He had been exposed to the elements. He had suffered scorching days and freezing nights with limited shelter, devastating tiredness due to lack of sleep, dehydration due to limited water, and starvation due to no food. He had fasted for a week and a half.

"During the forty days and forty nights Satan had tempted the Mentor. In the weakest moments of human existence, the Mentor teaches the lesson that it is possible to withstand the onslaughts and temptations of Satan. The Mentor had demonstrated, during the three temptations, how we should also withstand the most frequent temptations that people face.

"'If you are the Son of God, command that these stones become bread,' Satan had said, going for the weakest part first. He had known the Mentor was hungry and had tempted Him with hedonism. We are also tempted daily with hedonism. We want to know where our every meal will come from, that our hunger will be satiated, and that our every desire will be satisfied. The teaching is in how the Mentor responded by saying, 'It is written: Man shall not live by bread alone, but by every word that proceeds from the mouth of God.'

"The second temptation had involved human egoism. Satan plays on our search for power and our desire for popularity. After taking the Mentor up into the Holy City, Satan had put him on the pinnacle of the temple and said, 'If you are the Son of God, throw Yourself down. For it is written in the Bible: He shall give His angels charge over you, and, in their hands, they shall bear you up, Lest you dash your foot against a stone.' Satan knows the scriptures and will tempt us with it, as he had done with the Mentor. The Mentor had responded, 'It is written again: You shall not tempt the Lord your God.' The Mentor's approach to Satan had been with what was written. He had not become angry and He had not tried to defend God. This lesson is clear. Resist the temptation by knowing the scriptures. The Mentor had known that not all his students would be able to remember passages of the lessons. He had advised, 'If you cannot remember passages in the heat of temptation, just say: Satan, the battle is not mine but God's.'

"The Mentor's final temptation had involved the hunger to possess material goods, materialism. Satan had taken the Mentor up a high mountain where they could see all the kingdoms of the world in their full glory. Satan said, 'All these things I will give You if You will fall down and worship me.' Satan had also told the Mentor that all the glory and riches of the kingdom had been given to him and that he had the power to give it to the Mentor if He would worship him. 'Away with you, Satan! For it is written: You shall worship the Lord your God, and Him only you shall serve.' Satan, having been resisted, fled away. Only then did the King come to rescue the extremely tired and hungry Mentor.

"It was only after these tests of temptation in the wilderness that the Mentor felt that He was adequately prepared to teach others. Only then did He openly share His life experiences and positively impact the students he taught.

"The Mentor had faced a personal battle with the authorities of that time. He had openly called the

Pharisees hypocrites for sitting at banquets with posh clothes. He had accused them of not possessing the inner moral fiber they had proclaimed to have. The Pharisees disliked this and had sought revenge.

"The Mentor had eventually been brought to the Sanhedrin, rabbis appointed to sit and form a tribunal. He had been given the accusations: violating the law of the Sabbath Day by performing the miracle of healing a sick person; threatening to destroy the Temple of the Jews; banishing demons out of and away from people, which had been considered sorcery; and claiming to be the son of God, the Messiah.

"He had stood at the foot of Golgotha. He had faithfully obeyed and followed every instruction He had received from the King, and it had brought Him to the foot of this mountain. Diligently fulfilling His life's purpose had prepared Him for the final ascent. Climbing this mountain and reaching its pinnacle was going to be arduous and excruciatingly painful, but He knew he had to complete His final duty.

"His Forefather had said, 'If anyone desires to come after Me, let him deny himself and take up his cross and follow Me. For whoever desires to save his life will lose it, but whoever loses his life for My sake will find it. For what profit is it to a man if he gains the whole world and loses his soul?'

"He had ascended the mountain to Gethsemane, the blood caused by the thorny crown on His head had mixed with his sweat and dripped down his face and neck.

"At the top of the mountain, the Mentor faced the culmination of His life's purpose. Simon of Cyrene had walked next to the Mentor, carrying His cross.

## Teacher on the Mount

The Mentor had been mounted on the cross, held up by a nail through each wrist and each foot. The nails had been weak fasteners. He had to lift his body in an attempt to overcome gravity's downward force. The pain He experienced was excruciating. After six hours hanging on the cross, He sensed He had reached the mountain peak of His life's purpose. He had known He would die here.

"He had become thirsty, and His mouth was dry. He asked for something to quench His thirst. A group of Jewish women had mixed wine and frankincense, creating a concoction used to lessen the pain felt by the convicted who hung on the crosses. The women soaked the liquid with a sponge mounted on the stalk of a hyssop plant and then extended it to His mouth.

"Sensing the numbing liquid on the sponge lifted to His mouth, He refused to drink. He needed to feel every second of pain to be a pure offering for many. After climbing the darkest and most difficult mountain for almost nine hours, he cried out, 'Eloi Eloi lama sabachthani?' which means 'My God, my God, why hast thou forsaken me?'

"It had darkened around Calvary. Sensing the imminent storm, the soldiers had started breaking the bones of the men who were being crucified. The Mentor could not allow the soldiers to break His bones. His Father, the King, intervened.

"A blind Roman centurion, Longinus, had taken his spear and thrust it into the Mentor's side. As the spear entered the soft flesh and severed organs and arteries, the blood of the Mentor had splashed into Longinus' eyes. His blind eyes were healed by the blood from the perfect offering for all mankind, living and dead."

Abigail wipes the tears from her face as she considers the agonizing mountain the Mentor had to climb.

"May this insight allow you not only to climb physical mountains but also help you climb your proverbial mountains, too. Live a life of affluence and comfort, but also reach the pinnacle of your life purpose. Achieving this is harder than the physical climb because it requires you to overcome the peaks of the mind, the dualistic thinking, and the perspectives every person learns from an early age," Mrs. Watkins finishes.

Mrs. Watkins hands Abigail an envelope. "To climb a mountain like Everest, you require specific training in the correct techniques. This is a gift card for virtual-reality training sessions. You must climb a few simple mountains and learn basic mountaineering before taking these lessons."

"I don't know what to say," Abigail exclaims. "You have already done so much in helping me achieve my dream, and now this." New tears wet her cheeks, and she embraces the old lady.

# Chapter 18

## Heir of Fire

Sarah approaches the door to the Coffee Bean where a neatly-dressed young woman greets her with a friendly smile. "Welcome to the Coffee Bean. Table for one?"

As the lady opens the door, the aroma of fresh coffee hits Sarah, and she knows instantly why Mrs. Watkins wanted to meet her here. The quaint coffee shop was a community. Everyone smiled at her as she entered.

"I'm meeting someone here. I was instructed to ask for the booth at the back," Sarah grins.

"Ah, another of Mrs. Watkins's guests," the hostess smiles.

Since their telephone call, Sarah had read and written endlessly in the hopes of completing Mrs. Watkins's book before their meeting. She had decided to arrive early so that she might complete the book without distraction before meeting her.

After being seated in the cozy corner and placing her order, she opens the book at her bookmark and continues reading.

*"'The forefathers having heard this began all to revile him, saying: O all-devouring and insatiable! Open, that the King of glory may come in. David the prophet says: Dost thou not know, O blind, that I when living in*

*the world prophesied this saying: Lift up your gates, O ye rulers." Hesaias said: 'I, foreseeing this by the Holy Spirit, wrote: The dead shall rise up, and those in their tombs shall be raised, and those in the earth shall rejoice. And where, O death, is thy sting? Where, O Hades, is thy victory?'"*[19]

*Never has it entered my conscience that the dead shall rise up*, Sarah thinks as she takes her journal and a pen out of her bag so she can write down her thoughts.

"There is a distinction made in this passage between the living and the dead. More clearly now is the connection that exists between the living and the souls who have passed on into Hades, as is mentioned by Hesaias, where the dead shall rise out of their tombs, and the living will rejoice with them at the same time. The distance between the living and the dead feels further in the presence of sadness and longing to be with them. I know this very well after the death of my daughter. But now I see that it is my senses that cause the distance to feel even farther. I can't see her, hold her, hear her, touch her, but perhaps when I do the inner work on my soul to connect to Jesus again, the perceived distance between myself and her may decrease. This I now know; my daughter is safe, and her soul is free. I think I am selfish to want her back rather than being grateful to have had those few hours with her. I have become bitter and selfish."

Placing her pen on the table, she closes her eyes and breathes deeply before reading further.

*"There came, then, again a voice saying: Lift up the*

---

[19] Gospel of Nicodemus Part II, Chapter 5 (21)

*gates. Hades, hearing the voice the second time, answered and as if forsooth he did not know, and says: Who is this King of glory? The angels of the Lord say: The Lord strong and mighty, the Lord mighty in battle. And immediately with these words the brazen gates were shattered, and the iron bars broken, and all the dead who had been bound came out of the prisons, and we with them and the King of glory came in the form of a man, and all the dark places of Hades were lighted up.*

*"Immediately Hades cried out: We have been conquered: woe to us! But who art thou, that has such power and might? And what art thou who comest here without sin who art seen to be small and yet of great power, lowly and exalted, the slave and the master, the soldier and the king, who hast power over the dead and living? Thou wast nailed to the cross and placed in the tomb; and now thou art free, and hast destroyed all our power. Art thou then the Jesus about whom the chief satrap Satan told us, that through cross and death thou art to inherit the whole world?*

*"Then the King of glory seized the chief satrap Satan by the head, and delivered him to His angels, and said: 'With iron chains bind his hands and his feet, and his neck, and his mouth. 'Then He delivered him to Hades, and said: 'Take him, and keep him secure till my second appearing.'*[20]

*And Hades, receiving Satan, said to him: 'Beelzebul, heir of fire and punishment, enemy of the saints, through what necessity didst thou bring about that the King of glory should be crucified so that He should come here and deprive us of our power? Turn and see that not one of the dead has been left in me, but all that thou hast*

---

[20] Gospel of Nicodemus Part II, Chapter 6 (22)

*gained through the tree of knowledge, all has thou lost through the tree of the cross: and all thy joy has been turned into grief; and wishing to put to death the King of Glory, thou hast put thyself to death. For, since I have received thee to keep thee safe, by experience shall thou learn how many evils I shall do unto thee. O arch-devil, the beginning of death, root of sin, end of all evil, what evil didst thou find in Jesus, that thou shouldst compass his destruction? How hast thou dared to do such evil? How hast thou busied thyself to bring down such a man into this darkness, through whom thou hast been deprived of all who have died from eternity?"*[21]

Sarah turns to the last page; she reads the sentence penned there. *"Jesus, the King of Glory, is my Mentor, Mrs Watkins."*

She sits back, amazed by what the Mentor had done for the souls in Hades. She knows the Mentor will also fight for and guide the soul of her baby daughter. A few tears spill from her eyes, but she knows they are the last tears of bitterness and regret she will shed. It feels to her as though the last piece of her broken heart has been put back in place. She closes the book and sips her now-cool coffee.

Mrs. Watkins enters the Coffee Bean and makes her way to the back of the shop, chatting to clusters of people as she passes.

"Good morning, Sarah. Can I assume by the closed book, you have finished it?" Mrs. Watkins shuffles into the booth across from Sarah.

"Mrs. Watkins, it is so good to see you again in person. I have just finished it. I decided to arrive a bit early

---

[21] Gospel of Nicodemus Part II, Chapter 7 (23)

to read the final pages. I must say it has been one of the most transformational books I have ever had the privilege to read. Thank you for giving me a gift that is helping me heal from wounds and sadness," Sarah says with a gentle smile.

"I have another gift that will transform your life," Mrs. Watkins says. "I had shared with you over the phone how Joseph, even when his brothers had wanted to murder him and had sold him as a slave, had kept moving on to 'and then.' So, too, I want to share with you the three values my Mentor taught me, which will allow you to look ahead and, although you will never forget the pain of losing your daughter, you will be able to enjoy a fulfilled life. Let me start. Time is running out.

"The first value my mentor taught me was not to assign blame in situations you can't control, forgive in situations where blame can be assigned. Letting go of blame or forgiving somebody who has done you wrong will set your soul and mind free

"You blame the hospital staff because they should have done more to save her your daughter, as well as the doctors, should have picked up the condition before her birth. The condition your daughter was rare and fatal. There was no way they could have picked it up before her birth. They did everything they could feasibly do in the time they had. Let go of the blame.

"You blame God for not intervening and saving your daughter's life. God has His reasons, and we may never know what those reasons are. God is the easiest to blame and usually is the first to be blamed because there is no science or apparent reasoning behind what He does.

"Perhaps you blame yourself. Realize that there was nothing you could have done differently during your pregnancy. What you do have control over is how you have treated those around you. You have pushed them away. You haven't allowed them to give you the comfort you need. Forgive yourself so you may repair those relationships. That is the first transformational value.

"The second transformational value is to learn to love. You need to connect with that love again. Learn to love the God you have known from a very early age, love your neighbor, and learn to love yourself, too.

"That brings us to the third transformational value, and that is to serve. Have you heard of the five stages of grief introduced by the academic work performed by Elizabeth Kubler-Ross?"

"Yes, we learnt about it and use it in the hospital," Sarah replies. "The five stages of grief a person encounters after losing a loved-one are denial, anger, bargaining, depression, and eventually, acceptance. Sue said, 'I have experienced the first four stages, although not in that order, and I have even experienced some of the stages more than once. It is the final acceptance stage that I have not reached yet."

"Dear Sarah, let me tell you about a sixth stage that was developed after the death of Elizabeth Kubler-Ross by her academic partner David Kessler. He had felt deep grief over the passing of two sons. He also could not reach the acceptance stage and struggled with the Kubler-Ross stages of grief. It was while going through his grief that he found a light that did not take the pain or loss away, but allowed him some form of healing."

"David extended the five stages of grief to six by adding 'finding meaning'. People asked him if he had found closure after the passing of his sons, which he had not. What he had experienced and shared with the concept of finding meaning in life again was to learn to remember them with more love and less pain and then move forward in a manner that honors the loved one. For you, dear Sarah, I believe you are honoring your daughter by the service you are giving to your patients in your hospital.

"Reflect on these transformational values and find what is personally meaningful to you. It is not what others think should be meaningful. It is to find what brings the sparkle back to your eye and brings you joy again. Then your acts of service will bring honor to the life of your daughter.

"May these three transformational values with the book that you have worked through allow you to live a joyful life again," Mrs. Watkins concludes, while her eyes lock with Sarah's tear-filled eyes...

# Chapter 19

# Mountaineering Techniques

Living in Johannesburg, South Africa, the opportunity to train on high, snow-capped mountains is very limited, so Abigail has to find an alternative to gain some experience before climbing Everest. Her heart beats with excitement as she enters the very chic and modern virtual-experience center. She has booked a mountaineering training session in advanced mountaineering techniques, use of tools, and safety.

Virtual-reality has been explained to her as a simulation of reality displayed in three-dimensional images and effects that allows the person wearing a virtual-reality headset to see and feel the environment as being real.

"Welcome to Virtual Experience. My name is Sabastian," the young man behind the reception desk smiles. "You are in for a real treat. The virtual training you are going to experience is world-renowned. Mountaineers preparing to climb Mount Rainier in America, K2 on the Pakistan and Chinese border, and the infamous Everest, where the summit runs across the borders of Nepal and China, have refined their skills with our program. The positive feedback we receive from experienced and novice mountaineers makes us a leader in the field with this superb technology."

"Am I the only person doing the training," Abigail asks, a bit unsure of what to expect.

"We only train on a one-on-one basis, so it will be you and your guide, Jessica; she has summited Everest three times. She will be guiding you through the mountaineering techniques and safety session. She is waiting for you just outside the chamber over there."

Adrenaline rushes through Abigail's body as she approaches the brown-haired lady in her mid-thirties.

"Welcome to the mountaineering virtual-reality experience. I have carefully gone over the survey you completed in your application. Please join me in the chamber where we are going to get you suited up, discuss the equipment you will need to become familiar with, and I'll teach you the techniques you need to learn," Jessica explains. Abigail follows her into the chamber and, after gearing up, takes a seat on a bench as Jessica starts the session with an introduction.

"As a newcomer to the mountaineering world, I will teach you about the importance of the ice-axe. It is one of your best friends on the mountain and a vital part of your gear. The ice-axe is a balance and safety tool when ascending or descending the mountain. Apart from assisting with balance, it can be used as a self-arrest tool to stop an expected fall and as a brake when sliding downhill." She picks up the ice-axe and continues, pointing out the different parts. "The ice-axe consists of the pick, head, adze, leash, leash stop, shaft, and spike. The pick is used while climbing steep sections and ice falls. It is used in the overhead position to dig into the ice in conjunction with crampons while climbing. The pick is also the part used during the self-arrest or brake. The adze helps chop steps and assists with making tent platforms. Holding the head of the ice-axe allows you to use the axe as a cane which provides support and improved balance. The spike at the bottom digs into the ground to provide support and can be used as a rescue, should you slip.

"One of the greatest dangers of high mountains is to slip and fall. The ice-axe is a valuable tool while sliding down a mountain slope in the snow. Always make sure your axe is held on the uphill side of the mountain slope. If you find yourself sliding on your stomach with your head pointing up the mountain, take your axe and bring it into the control position. The adze should be over your left shoulder, gripped with your left hand, while the shaft is secured in your right hand and held close to your body. The right-hand holds the shaft close to the pelvic bone. Levelling up on the axe head, put your head over the axe's head to transfer more of your body's weight. Make sure to turn your face away to prevent facial damage that can be caused by the adze of the axe or the snow coming down the mountainside. Arch your back to allow even more of the body's weight on the axe head. Also, practice keeping your feet off the snow by flexing the knees and opening your legs. Be aggressive in trying to stop sliding further." Jessica demonstrates the moves as she explains them to Abigail.

"If you find yourself sliding on your back with your head pointing up the mountain, roll onto your stomach and repeat the basic stopping technique."

Abigail is handed the ice-axe. She slips the virtual-reality headset over her eyes. The rush of the howling wind fills her ears. The ground begins to slip from beneath her feet.

*Teacher on the Mount*

"I'm sliding!" Abigail screams.

"Use your ice-axe and the stopping technique I have taught you!" Jessica yells to be heard over the howling wind.

With heart hammering, Abigail comes to a stop. She stands up and cannot believe that this is only a virtual reality. The environment created feels so real! The adrenaline, the fear, and the relief when she came to a successful stop makes her quadricep muscles cramp.

"You handled the challenge very well," Jessica congratulates Abigail as she removes the headset. "Another way to stop is by braking. To brake, drive the shaft of the ice-axe hard into the ground. Be aggressive. Braking as fast as possible is the key to survival.

"However, these tips are only useful if you are sliding with your head pointing to the top of the mountain. Practice stopping and breaking a few more times, and we can move on to the more difficult technique."

As soon as Abigail slips the headset over her head, she feels the earth-shaking underneath her feet, and she loses footing. As quickly as possible, she gets the ice-axe into a useful position. Now knowing she needs to brake; she uses the new technique as fast as possible to bring her body to a stop. She practices a few more slides, waiting anxiously each time for the sudden vibrations which cause the slide.

"Well done! Your awareness of imminent danger and the speed of your reaction is excellent! Now you need to know what to do when you're sliding down the mountain with your head pointing down." Abigail puts the headset aside as she watches and listens to the demonstration.

"Put the axe out to one side of the body by extending the elbow as straight as possible. Apply pressure to the pike of the axe. Your feet will automatically start to move downwards. Push the head of the axe into the ground next to your hip, then try and sit up by pushing your feet and knees together while spinning around at the same time. This will move you onto your stomach where the basic control position can be used."

Abigail awaits the next slide and mentally rehearses what she has just learned. The slope starts shifting beneath her, and she starts sliding down the slope. Using the braking technique while sliding on her stomach does not go according to plan, and She continues to slide down the slope. A soft mattress breaks her fall at the base of the slope.

Jessica demonstrates the technique again and instructs her to try again. After the third attempt, Abigail manages to stop herself. Jessica makes her practice several more times before moving on. Abigail feels her muscles twitch as she stands up for what feels like the hundredth time.

"Remember, stopping and braking are to be used as a last resort," Jessica explains as they make their way to the next chamber. "It is best to learn proper balance, good footing, and how to use your tools to assist where needed.

"Practicing in a real setting is crucial. Take a mountaineering friend with when you practice and assess the safety of the mountain slope. Make sure the slope is not too steep and has a safe area where you can come to a natural stop if you are not successful in applying the ice-axe stopping and braking techniques. Don't wear crampons and ensure you don't have anything tied to you while you practice, as this can cause injury. A helmet is important to avoid head injuries.

"Trekking-poles are used exclusively for balance and are a nice-to-have, rather than an essential item. Trekking-poles are an individual choice. Some climbers prefer not to use trekking-poles and rely solely on the strength of their legs and their balance. My personal preference is to use trekking-poles. They are easily shortened and can be hung on the side of your backpack. On long hiking days, I find that the trekking poles help distribute weight evenly. The entire kinetic chain can be used without my legs becoming tired. In winter climbs where it has snowed during the night, trekking-poles can help as you trudge through knee-deep snow. However, as the incline steepens, it is crucial to replace the trekking-poles with the ice-axe. As I've already mentioned, the preferred position of the axe is in the uphill hand.

"Let's learn how to cut steps. It is possible to cut steps with the adze of the ice axe to ascend or descend a steep slope at sections where the ice is firm and when you do not have your crampons on. It is a decision that should be made carefully, and safety needs to be placed above all other considerations. In the instance where the sliding distance is minimal if you should slip and it is only a small distance of hard ice separating two softer snow areas on the slope, this technique can be used.

"Take the ice axe in the uphill hand with the adze facing forward and bend your knees. Hit the ice with the axe and take slices of ice away. It may be necessary to hit the ice a few times before a step is created. Ensure that the step is big enough for your foot. Angle the step that you are cutting so that it will hold your body weight. The leg on the downside of the slope will have to cross over the uphill leg slightly. When you become tired, simply cut a broader step so that both feet will fit. Take breaks and don't rush the process." Jessica leads her student to a large ice-wall, where she practices making steps.

She is then led to a chamber with an icy slope, and Jessica hands Abigail crampons with instructions on how to secure them. "Place the crampons, tips facing upwards, on the slope. Place the toe of your boot into the crampon, then secure the locking mechanism before tightening the strap." After making sure Abigail has secured her crampon correctly, she continues.

"There may be times when you encounter slopes where the ice is so slippery that hiking boots won't grip. Crampons must be used. Crampons are best kept in a bag to protect clothing and other equipment in the rucksack.

"Assess the ice before approaching it. If you feel you will need the crampons, find a place where the incline is not too steep. Practice attaching the crampons quickly while standing. Remain prepared at all times for a slide. Sitting down on a slope puts you off balance and leaves you unprepared." After Abigail practices with the crampons for a while, Jessica continues.

"Preparation, as always, is the key to success. Make sure the crampons you use fit your hiking boots perfectly. There should be no space between the boot and the crampon, and the toe piece should fit perfectly. Ensure the locking mechanism at the back is in working order. There should be no movement between the boot and the crampon. Don't leave the strap too long, as this may cause you to trip. Cut the strap to the right length.

"Techniques to walk with crampons need to be practiced. Walking on a flatter part of the slope is a good place to start practicing walking with crampons because it will be easy to place your foot flat down. As the incline of the slope increases, it will become increasingly more difficult to place the boot flat on the slope surface. It is then advised to place the boot with the toe facing down the slope and to the side while ascending, followed by the outside leg crossing the supporting leg. The steepness of the slope will determine how much the toe should face downward. The aim when traversing a slope should always be to place the crampon and boot flat down on the snow surface. To descend, avoid the temptation to use the normal heel to toe gait pattern but rather keep the toe of the boot flat which will allow all the points of the crampon to make contact with the snow at the same time. Almost assume a semi-lunge seated position with the leg that steps forward.

"Ascending steep slopes faster is possible by using the two front rows of the crampons and using the ice axe as a three-gait pattern. Keep the heel raised after you have kicked into the slope. It is hard work to keep the heel up, but it is more efficient." Abigail feels every muscle in her body, screaming as she continues practicing techniques from the lessons she has been given.

"For descending, turn your body upwards to the top of the mountain. This will make you feel safer than facing downward while descending. Again, kick the front points of the crampons into the slope and keep the heel up. Also, make use of the pike of the ice axe when the slope is extremely steep or when you feel insecure to descend on your hands and feet."

Jessica concludes the virtual-reality session with a final practice before escorting Abigail to the main area. "I must say that you have impressed me during the techniques. You can place all the gear in the corner there and meet me in reception for a debriefing session. You must have many questions which I will answer," Jessica says with a smile.

# Chapter 20

## Teacher on the Mount

Abigail and Sarah sit in the same booth of the Coffee Bean where they had met for several intimate teaching and mentoring sessions with Mrs. Watkins. Mrs. Watkins's son had requested the meeting this time. Without hesitation, Abigail and Sarah had accepted the invitation.

Sitting together at the table, they share the unique experiences they'd had and what they had learned from the inspirational Mrs. Watkins. They wait in anticipation, curious as to why their teacher had requested to meet with them together and why the invitation had been extended by her son.

"I can't believe it has been eight months since we last saw each other. After spending valuable time listening to her YouTube mountaineering videos, I joined a mountaineering club and have done some fairly low-grade climbs. I then went for virtual-reality technique training sessions to prepare for higher, more dangerous climbs. I have had the opportunity to gain experience, climbing at higher altitudes and over more-demanding terrain," Abigail gushes.

"Professionally, I have made big strides to complete my research study. Her advice to practice non-dualistic thinking in an ever-changing culture of diversity in South Africa has impacted the students I'm privileged to teach. The feeling that I'm right and they're wrong, and that there is only one correct perspective or answer to a problem, has changed to considering their viewpoints and answers. When I walk into a lecture hall, I am more cognizant of the fact that they bring their own unique experience with them into the lecture. When I refuse to see and notice this, I shut myself off from the students. There is a metaphorical wall that is gradually built between the facilitator and the students. In essence, the quotes Mrs. Watkins shared with me have had a tremendous impact on the way I teach.

"'Tell me and I'll forget. Teach me and I'll remember. Involve me and I'll learn.' This quote from Benjamin Franklin opened my eyes. Students don't only want to sit and listen to the knowledge that is thrown their way. They want to be involved. I have included blended learning, a mixture of face-to-face lectures, online activities, podcasts, and practical application, and the results have been mindboggling. This goes hand in hand with the following quotes: 'I never teach my pupils, I only provide the conditions in which they can learn,' by Albert Einstein and 'A good teacher is merely a catalyst,' by Bruce Lee. This quote by Mustafa Kemal Ataturk reminds me of Mrs. Watkins's Mentor: 'A good teacher is like a candle; it consumes itself to light the way for others.' We have some very interesting debates around the subjects we are discussing, and I have found that all my students, even the quiet ones, are fully engaged."

Sarah nods knowingly. "You could not be more correct," she begins. "Spending time with Mrs. Watkins was very confusing for me at first, but it has been a life-changing experience. It was just after 7 am when I entered the ward to start my shift. I heard a scream from Mrs. Watkins's room. She had been woken up by what seemed to be a nightmare. She immediately told me to cancel the operation. You can just imagine the chaos that ensued.

"Everyone was asking me to talk her out of cancelling the operation because of the level of pain she has had for the past three years. You know how long our knee and hip replacement list is and how the patients wait to get a new joint. What was especially strange was how she had wanted to go and climb a final mountain with her son, which wouldn't be possible without the knee replacement." Sarah recalls.

She tells Abigail about the death of her daughter and the blessing she had received from Mrs. Watkins in the form of a simple book. She explains how the small book has allowed her to talk about her loss without bitterness and resentment.

A man dressed in denim jeans and a tweed jacket approaches their table. He greets the two ladies.

"I was asked by my mother to come and read out a letter to you both," he explains. He clears his throat and tries to hide a deep sadness before reading a handwritten letter. 'My dear Therapist and Manager. Sadly, I will not join you today. I realized after the dream I had in the hospital the night before I cancelled my operation that I would not be with you for long. My decision to cancel the operation was from a deep belief that if I went ahead with the knee replacement procedure, I would not have had any time with you.

'In the dream, I was climbing at high altitude, ascending a beautiful, white ice slope towards the mountain peak. After reaching the peak, I was joined by my Mentor. He stood next to me, and we both looked down over the breathtakingly magnificent view. The highest mountains always give the best views once the summit is reached.'"

Abigail smiles and nods her head in agreement while the son continues to read. 'My Mentor met me atop the mountain and said to me: You have too much to do and too little time. There are people who need your assistance, and your time left on Earth is short. Embrace your pain and sacrifice yourself for the good of others, as I did.'"

Tears well in both Abigail and Sarah's eyes as they listen to the reason Mrs. Watkins had cancelled her knee operation. The realization dawns on them that she is no longer with them.

"'I want you to know that the Mentor who has been instrumental in my life and who has helped and guided me to reach the highest peaks personally, professionally, and in mountaineering is also your Mentor. He is always close and wants to have a deep personal relationship with you. He cares and helps. Just call out to Him, and He will answer. His answer can come in the light breeze blowing over a sandy shore or in the mighty wind blowing down a mountain slope. Other times, His answer is in the passages you read in books or the comforting words spoken by a dear friend.

'Don't be saddened by my death. The last eight months have been amazing. I had the privilege to share my experiences and knowledge while helping you both face what you needed to face. I was lucky enough to receive a warning about my imminent death which allowed me to prepare. I will always be close to you. Continue to grow and share what you have gained from our interactions. Share with those in need and comfort the sad and weary. Do this, and you will always remember me and the teachings of the Mentor.'"

Tears stream down the faces of the two ladies as their love for their teacher, Mrs. Watkins, fills their hearts.

"There are still two final tasks left for me to perform as asked by my mother. Two special gifts from her to you," the son continues as they wipe the tears from their faces. He hands them each an envelope, smiles sadly, and leaves.

"To my dear Therapist," Abigail reads. "Your enthusiasm for your profession, research, and mountaineering have warmed my heart. I found myself enjoying our moments together and looked forward to each new interaction. To you, I leave all my mountaineering equipment and clothes. Choose what you need and use it. I have been so pleased by your progress with your climbing skills and graded climbs. I believe you are ready. I have booked and paid for a Mount Everest expedition for you." Abigail looks at the attached plane ticket, dated for 31 March. "Know that the Mentor and I will be with you every step of the way.

"I have only one request. As you summit Mount Everest, will you take this list with you?" Abigail takes the folded paper out of the envelope and opens it.

'What I still have to do before my final hour' is written on the top of the page, followed by a tick list. Abigail notices that only one list item must be ticked off: stand on the summit of the highest mountain on Earth one more time with a friend.'

Abigail continues to read the letter. "I leave you with this: 'But those who wait on the Lord shall renew their strength; They shall mount up with wings like eagles, They shall run and not be weary, They shall walk and not faint.'" Fresh tears fill Abigail's eyes.

"My dear Manager Sarah," Sarah reads. "You supported me and helped me after I decided to cancel the operation. In you, I saw myself. I too, had lost a baby. My baby was stillborn. Seeing how you have healed and transformed your understanding of life and death has been inspirational. You rose out of the ashes like a phoenix, and I commend you for your tenacity. To you, I leave a contact number. I was overjoyed to hear you have reunited with your husband and are now trying, and struggling, to adopt a baby. Phone this number. I was able to find a young girl who is due to give birth shortly. I have been in contact with the necessary contacts, and they are eager to meet with you. You are first on their list. I leave you with this: 'do not be terrified, or afraid of them. The Lord your God, who goes before you, He will fight for you, according to all He did for you in Egypt before your eyes.'"

Abigail and Sarah embrace in consolation. The generosity and love Mrs. Watkins had shown them has reframed their hearts, souls, and lives.

# Chapter 21

# Reaching the Highest Mountains within Yourself

The South Col Route is only one of eighteen climbable routes up Mount Everest. It was climbed for the first time by the Sherpa Tenzing Norgay and Sir Edmond Hillary, a New Zealand beekeeper, during a 1953 British expedition.

Abigail had been shocked when she had opened the gift Mrs. Watkins had given her. The fully paid trip was for this infamous South Col Route. She had spent nine months preparing physically and mentally for this moment.

It is here on Mount Everest, at the death zone above 8000 meters, where the air is thin and stripped of oxygen, that Abigail is overwhelmed with emotion. The teachings and guidance from the silver-haired lady who had become her teacher have allowed her to see the peak of Mount Everest above her. Only 850 meters stand between her and the top of the world. As she rests before the final ascent, she reflects on her Everest journey.

A very important shift had occurred in her heart and soul. She has developed an understanding of the purpose of her life and what is truly important.

Before the start of the trip, the expedition leader, who had also been a close friend of Mrs. Watkins, had forwarded a musical piece to her phone. "I was asked to send you this song before you start the expedition. It may be the answer to the question you once asked about having to work so hard, always wanting more, and pushing yourself to gain material things," he had said.

Abigail had opened her phone and clicked the link for the song. The reference Isaiah 65: 21-23 rolled up and, to her surprise, a choir started singing the following words:

> *'They shall build houses, inhabiting them; and they shall plant vineyards, and eat of their fruit. They shall not build and another inhabit, they shall not plant and another eat.[22] They shall not labor, nor labor in vain, for they are the elect of the Lord, and they shall, shall build houses, inhabiting them, and eat the fruit of their labors; Mine elect shall long enjoy the work of their hands.'[23]*

These simple but impactful words calmed her heart and moved her soul. *The hard work I have put into following the King's voice will not be in vain*, she thinks. She had wiped her tears and started the hike to Base Camp.

During the hike to Base Camp, Abigail couldn't believe this was truly happening. Her dream of climbing the highest mountain on Earth had come true.

Base Camp, 5400 meters above sea level, is a busy international community filled with chatter in multiple languages. Tents are scattered everywhere, the latest technology is used to communicate the progress of

---

[22] Isaiah 65:21-22 NKJV

[23] Isaiah 65:21-23 (portions off) NKJV arranged into a song titled Fruit of their labours by Iain Johnson

climbers, weather forecasts are carefully watched, and buffalo meat is prepared by the Base Camp chefs.

In the hustle and bustle of Base Camp, the irony can be seen: the latest technological advancements alongside washing clothes by hand in freezing lakes; the excitement of starting the ascent to Camp One alongside the fear at the sound of thunderous avalanches as icefalls collapse; the immense joy of successful climbers returning from the top of Mount Everest alongside the devastating news of climbers who had lost their lives.

From Base Camp, a treacherous icefall, at 5500 meters, had to be surmounted. The Khumbu icefall was filled with danger at every step, the threat of an avalanche always present. Abigail remembers clicking into the ropes and moving as fast as possible through the treacherous terrain. On the ladder, the group had used ropes to give additional balance as icy winds had swept in and almost derailed them. Teamwork was a vital aspect of survival.

Camp One, at 5943 meters, had been a six-hour journey. Here, the stillness had overwhelmed the senses, and the terrain had felt increasingly unsteady. The echo of ice cracking deep beneath her tent had frightened her. She had prayed devoutly. She missed her family, and the fear of possibly never seeing them again hit her hard. Then grit and tenacity of mind kicked in. She realized she had to overcome this obstacle to move on, both literally and figuratively. Her many months of intensive preparation and the words of Mrs. Watkins pushed her on.

"Reaching the highest mountains will require you to reach deep within yourself, and you will need tenacity and a strong will. Now, learn and grow so that you can conquer any deep-seated perceptions, negative paradigms, and fears that will keep you back and make you crack on the mountain. Reaching the summit of Mount Everest takes every last drop of sweat, faith, and unwavering belief."

The journey from Camp One to Camp Two had taken two and a half hours. Constant fear of falling into a crevasse and hiking in the heat of the day had drained Abigail's energy. It had been a mental and physical challenge. Abigail had used wise words learned from Mrs. Watkins: "It is not about you, it is about looking up and doing it for others." Her fellow climbers had needed help as well, and she had provided support, motivation, and reliability as a mountaineering buddy. This had renewed her, giving her strength to continue onwards, up the Lhotse Face, to Camp Three.

The air had become increasingly thinner. They had not started using oxygen yet. Her body had to rely on months of altitude training. She had felt as though her airway was blocked. Dry coughs had been audible among the climbers.

Abigail and her climbing companions had made sure they were fastened to ropes before climbing up the hard, steep, icy angle at 7162 meters above sea level.

They had rested as much as possible at each camp, allowing their bodies a chance to recover. The increasing altitude was the only constant challenge.

In her tent at Camp Two, she had opened a letter from Sarah, who had become one of her dearest friends since the passing of their teacher. The letter contained historical wisdom and truth:

*'You whom I have taken from the ends of the Earth, and called from its farthest regions, and said to you. You are my servant, I have chosen you and have not cast you away: Fear not, for I am with you. Be not dismayed, for I am your God. I will strengthen you. Yes, I will help you, I will uphold you with My righteous right hand.'*[24]

From Camp Three it was a steep climb up limestone rock with a sustained grade. They had to start using oxygen now. After three hours, the steepness of the grade of the climb surprised Abigail. The surface of the Geneva Spur had been covered with enough snow to make the climb safer than the loose rocks. They had finally reached the South Col after an arduous climb.

Climbing at these heights, with her crampons secured to her boots, Abigail had continued with the reflective practice that had transformed her mind. The lessons from Mrs. Watkins had always been about what her Mentor had taught her. It was here, in the harshest conditions and altitudes not conducive to human life, that she had felt a deep closeness to the Mentor. He had been an ever-present help and support in her time of need.

They had continued, step by step, on the South Col, 8016 meters above sea level. Here, the ground under their feet had flattened out, and they had been walking on loose rock. It had felt like a moon-walking expedition. They had set up tents here. The views of Everest to the north and Lhotse to the south were breath-taking.

The Sherpas, the unsung heroes, moved busily

---

[24] Isaiah 41:9-10

around in preparation for the summit. They have had time to rest before their time of departure.

At 23:00 they don their final gear, and they step into the darkness, setting off on an arduous five-hour climb to the peak. They make their slow ascent up the Triangular Face and Balcony in a long line, with headlamps lighting the way in the dark. Abigail walks on, one foot in front of the other, step by step.

Abigail's mind wanders to the Sarah and how her life has been completely transformed since meeting Mrs. Watkins and hearing about the Mentor. The two of them had one last coffee together, meeting at the Coffee Bean, where they had always met Mrs. Watkins, just before the start of the Everest journey. Meeting at the coffee shop had become a once-a-month treat which she always looked forward to.

This last meeting had been exciting as Sarah walked in carrying her new-born adopted daughter. Sarah's eyes sparkled as she shared her newfound insight while reflecting on her darkest moments. An analogy of a mountain ascent was used in her reflection.

"After the passing of my baby daughter, I went through the typical stages of grief after loss: denial and isolation, anger, bargaining, and depression, but I couldn't accept. I isolated myself by pushing away the person closest to me, my husband. I was angry, and I felt so alone. My anger was directed at the King and the Mentor. How could They have allowed this to happen? I started denying my faith and fell into a deep depression. Every step was difficult. The loneliness was made worse by what I thought were insensitive comments made by family, friends, and colleagues. It seemed as though they could not understand why time did not make it better or why I was pushing everyone away. They honestly did make every effort they could to help me, but I was too angry and depressed to see it. I was unable to accept the loss of my daughter. It was a daily struggle to get out of bed and go to work, to carry on as normal. It felt as if the ascent to sanity, healthy relationships, and faith was never-ending.

"Climbing a known mountain peak and climbing through life's struggles and suffering are vastly different. The peak of a mountain like Mount Everest is known because the paths have been travelled before and you know what to expect. Things have been put in place to assist with the climb.

"During my ascent, the paths were untraveled. No textbooks or internet searches can prepare the climber. Abigail, can you remember how our teacher often talked about her Mentor? I had a personal encounter with the Mentor after reading the book she gave me. It was only when I stopped the self-pity, stopped the anger, and stopped blaming Him for the death of my daughter that I was able to reach the peak of my mountain. I now realize that the mountain of suffering and loss was the mountain I had to climb to reach the fullest and truest version of myself and the purpose of my life.

"Although the ascent was excruciatingly painful and lonely, littered with loss, bitterness, betrayal, hardship, and tears, I now know that I was never alone. The Mentor, who has always been fond of climbing the highest mountains in Jerusalem to seek stillness and closeness to the Creator and His Father, knows what suffering is. He had been hungry and tired. He had been betrayed by his closest friends. He had been tempted for forty days in a desert, persecuted by the people of his own culture, mocked, beaten with whips, and ultimately crucified on Calvary. Who better to trust as a companion than someone who has been through unthinkable suffering?

"What I learnt from His climbing and suffering is that He had always served others afterwards. His purpose in life was, and is, to serve all mankind, living or dead, with love. The book is very clear about what happens after this life, and the love of the Mentor, how He cared enough to go into the depths of Hades to free the suffering of others. Death could not hold Him. Who better to trust when you feel like the mountain is too hard to climb? I realized that He has always been close and has always looked after me, encouraging me to reach the top of the mountain so that I would serve others on the descent. Others have lost a child or loved one and have been unable to cope with the loss. It is my life purpose to connect with them, to share my healing journey. It isn't about me; it's about others.

"When I was depressed, I was very selfish and lived only inside my thoughts, needs, and emotions. I was so consumed by the darkness that it never crossed my mind to look up and reach out to others who were going through the same pain and loss. So, go and achieve your dream of climbing Mount Everest, but know that you need to climb another mountain to reach the purpose of your life to serve others."

Abigail climbs on with her team close by. The oxygen bottles have been changed to ensure they have ample supply to reach the summit. She breathes deeply, taking in as much life-giving oxygen as she can. She feels Mrs. Watkins and the Mentor place a hand on each of her shoulders and her fatigue abates. Although she still must discover what her life purpose is, she can now clearly see what does not matter.

They continue the steep, technical climb to the South Summit, 8690 meters. The views of Lhotse are indescribable.

She has learned that she does not only live for herself – achieving her goals – but she lives to be of service to others. She has come to realize that negative thoughts do not serve her. They are merely Satan's attempt to distract her from what she can do to serve others. She has also learned that character is more important than comfort.

They cross the section between the South Summit and the well-known Hillary Step, which has changed since the days of Tenzing Norgay and Edmond Hillary. With less than an hour of moderately-steep climbing through snow, adrenaline keeps the climbers'-tired bodies going.

Finally, they reach the summit! Abigail surveys the surrounding views from the highest point on Earth before raising her arms and looking up to thank the Mentor and the King. She takes Mrs. Watkins's list from her pocket. With paper in hand, she closes her eyes, raises the paper to the sky, and says a prayer of thanks to the Mentor, the King, and Mrs. Watkins. As the sun begins to peek over the horizon, she ticks off the last item.

She has come to know the Creator of Earth intimately during the toughest physical, mental, and spiritual feat of her life. She recites Psalm 8:1-9 loudly, "*O Lord, our Lord, how excellent is Your Name in all the Earth. Who have set Your glory above the heavens! Out of the mouth of babes and nursing infants, You have ordained strength, because of Your enemies, that You may silence the enemy and the avenger. When I consider Your heavens, the work of Your fingers, the moon and the stars, which You have ordained. What is a man that You are mindful of him, and the son of man that You visit him? For You have made him a little lower than the angels, and You have crowned him with glory and honor. You have made him have dominion over the works of Your hands; You have put all things under his feet. All sheep and oxen - even the beasts of the field, the birds of the air, and the fish of the sea that pass through the paths of the seas. O Lord, our Lord. How excellent is Your name in all the earth!"*

The End or is it the Beginning...

# ABOUT KHARIS PUBLISHING

**KHARIS PUBLISHING** is an independent, traditional publishing house with a core mission to publish impactful books, and channel proceeds into establishing mini-libraries or resource centers for orphanages in developing countries, so these kids will learn to read, dream, and grow. Every time you purchase a book from Kharis Publishing or partner as an author, you are helping give these kids an amazing opportunity to read, dream, and grow. Kharis Publishing is an imprint of Kharis Media LLC. Learn more at https://www.kharispublishing.com.

www.ingramcontent.com/pod-product-compliance
Lightning Source LLC
Chambersburg PA
CBHW070157100426
42743CB00013B/2947